Human rights

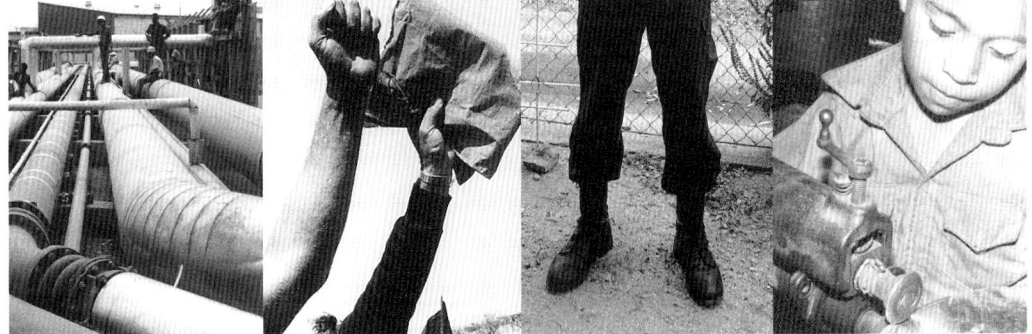

is it any of your business?

Amnesty International   The Prince of Wales Business Leaders Forum

Human rights – is it any of your business?

Authors: Peter Frankental and Frances House
Case study researchers: Aidan Davy and Raj Thamotheram
Designer: Alison Beanland
Printed by Folium
Photographs from Panos Pictures

© Amnesty International UK and The Prince of Wales Business Leaders Forum
April 2000

Amnesty International UK
99-119 Rosebery Avenue
London EC1R 4RE
United Kingdom
Tel: 44 (0)20 7814 6200
Fax: 44 (0)20 7833 1510
www.amnesty.org.uk/business

Amnesty International's mandate is to promote
the values of the Universal Declaration of
Human Rights and to work worldwide for the
release of prisoners of conscience, for fair trials
for political prisoners and for an end to torture,
extrajudicial executions, 'disappearances' and
the death penalty. Amnesty International is
independent of any government, political
persuasion or religious creed.

The Prince of Wales Business Leaders Forum
15-16 Cornwall Terrace
London NW1 4QP
United Kingdom
Tel: 44 (0)20 7467 3600
Fax: 44 (0)20 7467 3610
www.pwblf.org

The Prince of Wales Business Leaders Forum is an
international charity which was founded in 1990 to
promote socially responsible business practices that
benefit business and society, and which help to
achieve socially, economically and environmentally
sustainable development. The Forum works with
over 50 of the world's leading multinational
companies, and is active in some 30 emerging
and transition economies.

Product code: PB179
ISBN: 1-873328-43-5

This publication is intended to provide terms of reference to companies seeking to address the human rights context of their
operations. The case studies are presented from the perspective of the companies featured and are based primarily on
information provided by them. The recommendations reflect an evolutionary process rather than a definitive statement of policy.
Nothing in this document is intended to serve as a judgement on or as an endorsement of the human rights record of any of the
companies profiled.

Contents

PART II   Company case studies

PART III   Resources

Foreword

"One of the greatest ironies of this period in history is that, just as technology remakes our world, the need to maintain the human dimension of our work, and a company's sense of its social responsibility, is growing at an equally rapid pace. Harmonising economic growth with the protection of human rights is one of the greatest challenges we face today."

**Mary Robinson
UN High Commissioner for
Human Rights**
Davos, February 2000

"Big companies need to step into the breach to ensure that globalisation delivers more than a litany of dashed hopes. We must now act as co-guarantors of human rights."

**Göran Lindahl
President and CEO of ABB**

Why do human rights matter to business? The globalisation of the world economy in the post-Communist era offers unprecedented opportunities to business. Consumer goods industries source from an ever-increasing number of suppliers in developing countries and transitional economies. The extractive industries now have investment options which were previously denied them by political or ideological barriers.

But with rapidly escalating opportunity come unprecedented levels of threat, as companies find themselves caught up in situations of conflict and human rights violations which are the context for their operations in many countries today. These constitute a threat to the stability of the investment climate, to the physical security of employees and installations, and to corporate reputation if companies lack appropriate policies and practices which today's informed and critical society expects of them. The pressures on transnational companies to avoid doing harm and to exercise their legitimate influence for good are growing.

Responsible companies have long understood a duty of care towards their employees. More recently, they have accepted that the bounds of their responsibility should be extended to embrace protection of the environment. Today, civil conflict and human rights violations present them with new challenges and dilemmas for which few have shown themselves prepared, but which, ignored or badly handled, have proved hugely damaging to reputation.

The purpose of this publication is to inform companies on the human rights problems they may confront and to assist them in developing policies which will help both to protect themselves and improve the context in which they work. For the first time in modern history, a framework of international values exists which can help shape company policy. So too can the example of a growing number of leading transnational companies on whose experience we have drawn.

Companies cannot and should not be the moral arbiters of the world. They cannot usurp the role of government, nor solve all the social problems they confront. But their influence upon the global political economy is growing and their presence increasingly affects the societies in which they operate. With this reality comes the need to recognise that their ability to continue to provide goods and services and create financial wealth – in which the private sector has proved uniquely successful – will depend on their acceptability to an international society which increasingly regards protection of human rights as a condition of the corporate licence to operate.

**Sir Geoffrey Chandler
Chair, Amnesty International UK Business Group
and former Shell senior executive**
April 2000

HUMAN RIGHTS – is it any of your business?

Executive summary

The question of human rights is age-old, as is the practice of business. And yet the two issues are only just beginning to be seen as inextricably linked. Transnational companies which are making genuine attempts to operate responsibly in this field are, to a large extent, entering uncharted territory where codes of conduct proliferate and interpretations vary. This publication does not claim to be a definitive guide to this field, but it does offer a comprehensive and practical introduction to a subject now on the agenda of responsible companies and at the forefront of public attention. It is targeted primarily at those who formulate policy and at operational managers of transnational companies, tackling the question of human rights from Board level through to working with sub-contractors. It addresses the human rights issues and dilemmas that affect companies across most of their functions and throughout their organisational structure. It takes as its point of departure the Universal Declaration of Human Rights which calls upon 'every individual and organ of society' to uphold these internationally accepted standards.

What does this primer offer?

- a rationale and a guide for companies to develop and implement human rights policies

- practical recommendations for good corporate practice, drawing on case studies from selected transnational companies

- a survey of the current landscape facing transnationals where a wide range of influences are having an impact on the company's reputation with regard to its human rights performance

- an overview of useful initiatives, codes and guidelines which may help a company wanting to put into practice a commitment to uphold human rights standards

PART I

1. Overview:

Human rights are now seen as an integral part of responsible business. The internationally accepted framework for human rights is the UN's Universal Declaration of Human Rights. This framework should form the basis of a company's human rights policy and strategy for implementation in all its legitimate spheres of influence. Companies operating in countries where serious human rights violations occur are under heightened scrutiny from local communities, non-governmental organisations (NGOs), consumer groups and the media. These companies will find that a human rights policy, underpinned by full support from the Board and appropriate organisational positioning, is an essential element of sound risk management and reputation assurance. Human rights are becoming a bottom-line business issue. A corporate commitment to upholding international standards can bring benefits to companies and society at large.

2. Risks and dilemmas:

Transnational companies face innumerable dilemmas in many countries where they have a presence: investing in areas of conflict which pose security threats to property and personnel; taking investment decisions under an incumbent democratic government which is later overthrown by a dictatorship; operating in countries where freedom of information and expression are denied to citizens; paying taxes to corrupt and undemocratic administrations which may allocate more state revenue to the military than to basic health and education services. These situations carry with them serious human rights risks for companies. The primer recommends a series of steps companies can take to minimise the negative impact of their presence in such situations and to maximise the positive impact. It draws lessons from the experiences of a number of transnational companies. (See Part II for case studies.)

- Revenue allocation and corruption
- Operating in conflict zones
- Use of security forces
- Land rights/indigenous peoples' rights
- Labour rights: – freedom of association
                      – child labour
                      – working conditions
                      – bonded and forced labour

3. Principles to practice:

A commitment to uphold international human rights standards in companies' business principles or codes of conduct is a good starting point, but companies need to go further. To win credibility from society at large, they must demonstrate top-level support, allocation of responsibility and resources to integrate human rights into mainstream business activities, ongoing stakeholder [1] consultation, independent verification and reporting against benchmarks. Human rights criteria must be included in contractual agreements with business partners. The primer recommends steps to be taken, drawing lessons from companies at varying stages along this path. (See Part II for case studies.)

4. Drivers of change:

Companies are facing pressure from many directions to demonstrate responsible business in their daily operations around the world. The primer summarises important drivers of change pertaining to human rights of which companies should be aware.

● Shareholder pressure:

Ethical and socially responsible investment is gaining momentum through increasing shareholder awareness of human rights issues and through changing legislation.

● Transparency and disclosure:

The technological revolution of the Internet and satellite communications means that companies have little, if any, hiding place. Individual citizens, community groups, local and international NGOs now have the potential to monitor more easily a company's practices in any given location and to communicate concerns or protests instantly where they perceive irresponsible corporate behaviour. Companies can use the Internet as part of their wider consultation process and to elicit feedback from interested parties.

● Social reporting and auditing:

Just as companies report on their environmental performance, so they should on their social performance, of which a respect for human rights is a cornerstone. A sound human rights policy should commit a company to both internal monitoring and independent auditing and reporting against stated objectives. This is important in assessing progress and identifying areas for improvement. It is essential that a company demonstrate transparency and accountability in this area in order to build trust and credibility with employees and stakeholders alike. The primer looks at frameworks for social auditing and reporting which may be of value to companies.

● Regulatory pressure:

Government regulation to ensure corporate responsibility is on the increase in Europe and the US. Companies need to be aware of their own legal obligations as well as aspects of international law which relate to corporate activity. There is a growing framework of compliance, reinforced by, *inter alia*, ILO conventions, European Union regulations, selective purchasing laws in the US, London Stock Exchange requirements.

1. 'Stakeholders' are defined in this publication as those contributing to the success of the business, which includes shareholders and employees, and those affected by its operations – which would include local communities and customers.

● **Normative pressure:**

There is a growing number of codes of conduct, guidelines and principles to which companies are being called upon by the UN, OECD, NGOs and others to adhere. While not legally binding, they are raising expectations within society at large about norms of responsible business worldwide. A number of NGOs and companies have embarked upon sector-wide or cross-sector initiatives to confront some of the challenges of implementation collectively to the mutual benefit of all parties.

PART II: Case studies

The case studies illustrate that there are no easy answers to human rights challenges. Companies in all sectors face risks and dilemmas, some more overt than others. The companies profiled have all recognised that human rights are a core business issue. Approaches vary and progress is mixed, but there are valuable lessons to be learned for other companies facing similar challenges.

Risks and dilemmas

These case studies explore how a number of companies are tackling major human rights challenges in their business:

- Use of security forces: the case of Shell in Nigeria
- Land rights/indigenous peoples' rights: the case of WMC Resources in the Philippines
- Labour rights: – freedom of association: the case of Reebok in Indonesia
     – child labour: the case of Pentland Group in Pakistan
     – working conditions: the case of B&Q in India
     – bonded and forced labour

Principles to practice

These case studies consider various processes by which companies are trying to put their human rights principles into practice:

- BP Amoco – exerting positive influence?
- Rio Tinto – facing the challenge of implementation
- Levi Strauss – forming multi-stakeholder partnerships

Part III: Resources

The primer concludes with a checklist for good corporate practice in human rights. It provides a list of resources – organisations, websites and publications – which may be of value to companies as they seek to integrate human rights into mainstream business planning and operations, into relations with business partners and host communities, and into dialogue with government representatives.

Summary of recommendations and key considerations

Transnational companies operating in or sourcing from countries with, repressive governments, ethnic conflict, a weak rule of law or poor labour standards, face serious risks to their reputation if they are seen to be complicit in human rights violations. The dilemmas posed by seeking to conduct responsible business in such environments gives rise to many challenges.

The areas for consideration highlighted below do not represent a comprehensive survey of the human rights field. Nor do they prescribe 'quick fix' solutions to deep-rooted problems. They do, however, offer companies some pointers and practical advice as to how to begin tackling systematically some of the most problematic risks and dilemmas associated with human rights. Human rights protection is the business of business, just as it is of every individual and organ of society. It is a matter of upholding international standards, maintaining corporate reputation and licence to operate, managing risk, and contributing to a stable investment climate based on equitable, sustainable development.

Integrating human rights into company operations

A corporate human rights strategy:

- Incorporate an explicit commitment to support the Universal Declaration of Human Rights and core ILO standards in the company's business principles and operations. This commitment must be explicitly endorsed by the Board.

- Assign responsibility to a senior manager for developing and mainstreaming the human rights strategy and for addressing complementary or potentially conflicting internal company policies.

- Conduct wide-ranging internal and external consultation with management and employees, local and international NGOs and community groups in developing the human rights policy. This would include consultation on practical guidelines for staff on implementation and performance indicators.

- Communicate the strategy and implementation plan to all parts of the business and to all business partners. Ensure the strategy is available in local languages.

- Conduct training for HQ and country staff to raise awareness of human rights. Include business partners in the training wherever possible. Engage independent NGOs, human rights experts to provide input to the training.

- Incorporate human rights criteria into the social impact assessment process. This should be an integral part of the pre-investment risk analysis in new areas of potential operation.

- Require country managers to demonstrate that they have apprised themselves of the human rights situation in their country, and of the means by which the company could proactively seek to have a positive impact on human rights, for example through an annual letter of assurance to the Board.

- Establish procedures for country managers in the event of staff being arbitrarily arrested, detained or subjected to other miscarriages of justice according to international standards.

- Establish on-going dialogue with relevant NGOs or local authorities where possible on the question of improving human rights protection. Cross-sector partnerships offer potentially powerful mechanisms for developing and implementing human rights strategies. The potential for such partnerships with NGOs or community groups should be explored at various levels, from investment decision-making through to local monitoring of human rights conditions or peace-building initiatives.

- Establish mechanisms of internal and independent monitoring and reporting on the company's compliance with its human rights commitments in all part of its operations.

- Raise human rights concerns with government authorities either unilaterally or collectively with other companies. Senior managers should be prepared to speak out where abuses persist and quiet diplomacy has failed. In developing policies and practices with regard to human rights, companies need to delineate clearly the boundaries of their responsibilities, their willingness to become involved in advocacy and exert influence. This clarifies the extent of assumed responsibilities and makes it possible to monitor progress against objectives and targets.

Conflict zones

Transnational companies in conflict zones may exacerbate hostilities by their presence and the economic impact of their operations. On the other hand, they may ameliorate the situation through contributing to economic development and reconciliation. In either case, their operations, employees, reputation are all likely to be at risk. Human rights are at the core of the risks and challenges facing companies operating in conflict-prone areas.

Companies operating in conflict zones:

Building on the recommendations for a corporate human rights strategy indicated above, the following considerations are important in relation to conflict situations;

- Preparation – in-house training, develop guidelines for staff operating in conflict zones.

- Dialogue and consultation – with a range of stakeholders on a systematic and on-going basis.

- Conduct screening of security forces where possible – follow guidelines issued by Human Rights Watch and Amnesty International UK.

- Partnerships – working collectively with other companies, NGOs, community groups and government bodies on specific development/reconciliation projects, such as small enterprise promotion. Collective action is often a more realistic option for a company operating in a politically sensitive environment than risking the exposure of unilateral approaches to the government.

- Evaluation and accountability – internal and independent monitoring, reporting and verification of compliance with human rights commitments, encompassing all those affected by the company's operations.

- Policy/advocacy with the government – possibly with other companies and stakeholders on issues related to conflict prevention or resolution.

- Creating enabling frameworks – working with other companies, government bodies, civil society, academia to build frameworks to address the causes of conflict. These can include advocacy for good governance and anti-corruption measures, participation in infrastructure projects, training for local civil society organisations.

Security forces

Companies using state or private security forces:

- Companies should insert a clause into any security agreement signed with the government or any state entity that requires, as a condition of contract, that state security forces operating in the area of company installations conform to the human rights obligations the government has assumed under the International Covenant on Civil and Political Rights, and other international human rights norms.

- Companies' security agreements with state entities should be made public with the sole exception of operational details that could jeopardise individuals' lives.

- Companies should screen the military and police who are assigned for their protection. They should seek to ensure that no soldier or police agent credibly implicated in human rights abuse be engaged in their protection.

- Careful background checks should be undertaken to ensure that former police or military officers who work as private contractors or as part of company security staff have no history of human rights abuses or paramilitary involvement.

- Companies must make absolutely clear to the police and military defending them – as well as to company staff and sub-contracted personnel – that human rights violations will not be tolerated, and that companies will be the first to press for investigation and prosecution if any abuses occur.

- Whenever credible allegations of human rights abuses surface, companies should insist that any soldiers and officers implicated be immediately suspended and the appropriate internal and criminal investigations launched.

- Companies should actively monitor the status of the investigations and press for resolution of the cases. If the investigations or prosecutions are stalled, companies should publicly condemn the failure to conduct or complete the investigations.

- Any material assistance given by companies to security forces must be non-lethal, and subject to external auditing.

Land rights and indigenous peoples' rights

Companies operating in areas where indigenous peoples have particular land rights:

- Base company principles on ILO Convention No. 169 on Indigenous and Tribal Peoples.

- Develop an understanding of indigenous peoples' perspectives and way of life. This is the starting point for respecting human rights in areas where indigenous peoples have a close attachment to ancestral territories, unique languages and dependency on subsistence agriculture.

- Develop an understanding about land tenure in the vicinity of operations, and of the threats to ancestral lands. In many situations, indigenous peoples do not enjoy security of tenure. In such situations, the potential for infringement of the rights of indigenous peoples is high. This should be factored into decision-making.

- Strive to achieve free and informed consent of indigenous peoples to proceed with developments on their ancestral lands, irrespective of whether companies are legally obliged to do so. While this may involve a high degree of consultation and community participation, the longer-term benefits to projects are worthwhile. This also applies to other situations (such as remote areas) where communities may be particularly vulnerable to the adverse consequences of large-scale developments.

- Be aware of the wealth of traditional knowledge that indigenous communities may have that is relevant to project decision-making and operations. The basis for helping to protect indigenous peoples' rights is mutual understanding and participatory decision-making.

Labour rights

The following labour rights issues are not an exhaustive list. They are those which, to date, have proved most problematic for companies operating in or sourcing from developing countries.

Building the right to freedom of association into a company's labour practices:

- Base company principles on ILO Convention No. 87 on the Freedom of Association and Protection of the Right to Organise, and No. 89 on the Right to Organise and Collective Bargaining.

- Incorporate company principles into all contracts with joint venture partners and sub-contractors, and build these principles into monitoring of business partners' practices.

- Ensure workers are aware of their rights through making company principles available in local languages. Arrange for oral briefings where illiteracy is a problem.

- Improve levels of worker communication and empowerment through adopting an explicit Worker Communication system which allows for safe reporting of grievances.

- Protect the safety of the worker and union representatives by providing confidential reporting mechanisms and monitoring.

- Demonstrate active follow-up of reported grievances and cases of harassment or discrimination.

- Be prepared to raise concerns of employee persecution by state authorities with relevant government officials through quiet diplomacy or speaking out when the need demands.

- In countries where union activity is illegal, explore means of alternative worker representation systems within the factory or installation. Consult with international and local NGOs and labour organisations as to appropriate frameworks. Establish partnerships where useful.

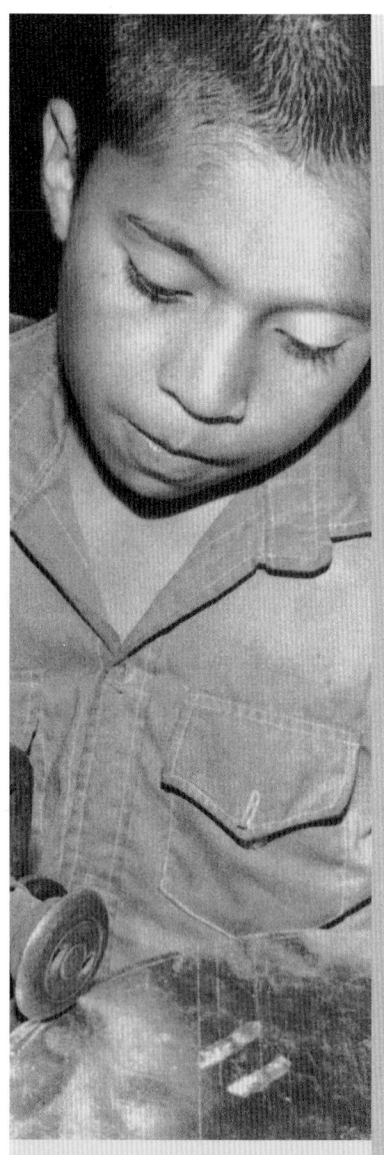

Dealing with the problem of child labour:

- Take, as a starting point, the UN Convention on the Rights of the Child, ILO Convention No. 182 and ILO Recommendation No. 190, both on The Worst Forms of Child Labour.

- As part of pre-investment risk assessment, consult widely with international and local NGOs and other community organisations on approaches to reducing and eventually eliminating the problem of child labour in the particular localities where the company is operating.

- Incorporate company principles into all contracts with joint venture partners and sub-contractors, and build these principles into monitoring of business partners' practices.

- Establish cross-sector partnerships with NGOs, private sector and government where possible to address the problems collaboratively. Local ownership of such initiatives is likely to make them more sustainable and successful. These initiatives may include flexible education provision for working children, childcare provision for working mothers, vocational training schemes for family members to boost employment opportunities of those of working age.

- Seek company commitment at the highest level to advocate responsible business in the area of child labour. If the CEO is not willing to speak out about the company's position on this issue, NGOs and the media are likely to question the company's real commitment to tackling the problem.

- Set up systems for regular internal and independent monitoring, verification and reporting.

- Provide training for staff internally to be aware of how to tackle the challenges of child labour in a variety of situations, such as dealing with joint-venture partners, opposition from local authorities, criticism from local NGOs or pressure groups. Consider bringing in relevant NGOs and others to provide elements of the training or briefing.

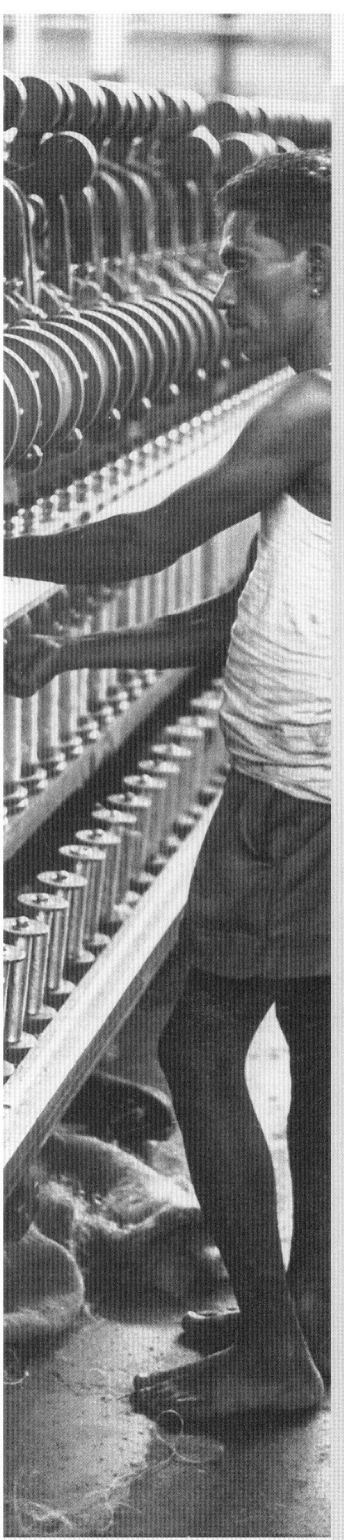

Companies addressing working conditions:

A company's influence over working conditions obviously lessens as it moves away from its direct operations to joint venture partners and sub-contractors down the supply chain. Nevertheless, society at large will hold a company responsible for violations occurring in plants from which it sources products or services, and therefore over which it has a degree of influence.

- Labour rights under the umbrella of 'working conditions' range from health and safety to fair wage provision. When drawing up company principles and guidelines, take into account ILO Convention No. 155 on Occupational Health and Safety, No. 131 on Minimum Wage Fixing, and be aware of the debate among unions, NGOs and governments on what constitutes a 'living wage'. Other ILO conventions cover issues such as discrimination, treatment of women, right to leisure time. They provide a good basis on which to build a company human rights policy.

- Incorporate company principles into all contracts with joint venture partners and sub-contractors, and build these principles into monitoring of business partners' practices.

- Ensure workers are aware of their rights through making company principles available in local languages. Arrange for oral briefings where illiteracy is a problem.

- Improve levels of worker communication and empowerment through adopting an explicit Worker Communication system which allows for safe reporting of grievances.

- Consult with international and local NGOs and labour organisations to explore possibilities of partnership initiatives to finding solutions to problems, such as micro-credit schemes for financially insecure homeworkers far down the supply chain.

- Consider working collaboratively with other companies and relevant government ministries in the sector to raise labour standards.

- Consult regularly from the outset with local management as to how to achieve continuous improvement and, therefore, competitiveness. Encourage a sense of local ownership by the factory or site manager to avoid being perceived as imposing solutions from the outside.

- Use external verification and monitoring to ensure continuous improvement within core operations and down the supply chain. Relevant NGOs can provide useful skills and independence in this work.

Bonded and forced labour:

There is no simple guide to identifying the use of bonded or forced labour, but companies need to be aware of the risks when monitoring suppliers for acceptable labour standards. The following pointers may be of help:

- ILO Convention No. 29 on Forced Labour provides an important starting point for companies operating in countries where forced or bonded labour is known to be a problem.

- Companies must develop checking procedures that involve good consultation and co-operation with local trade unions and NGOs working in the neighbourhood of their suppliers. Only in this way can companies obtain a detailed understanding of employment practices covering the localities, factories and suppliers in question. Indications that wages and/or working hours are linked to the repayment of loans or advances on wages should be seen as a danger signal, requiring detailed investigation. Wide-ranging consultation is an essential element of the pre-investment risk assessment and on-going monitoring of the situation.

- Companies should be aware that bonded labour can also be involved when suppliers claim that all workers are self-employed. Consultation with community organisations and NGOs is essential in investigating this risk.

- Companies operating in countries where bonded or forced labour is known to be a problem should undertake extensive stakeholder consultation and independent monitoring of the company's operations. Where possible, this should be undertaken with joint venture partners and sub-contractors as well.

- Country managers should also be prepared to raise concerns regarding bonded labour directly with the host government at an appropriate level. Acting collectively with other companies to raise concerns with the government lessens the risk to the individual company.

- Training for buyers and suppliers on this issue is important in order to raise awareness of the risks to the company, as well as to identify solutions to the problem. Relevant NGOs have a useful role to play in this training process.

The sections which follow set out the rationale and context for a company to address human rights at various stages in its operations, drawing on the experience of a number of transnational companies operating in or sourcing from developing countries.

HUMAN RIGHTS – is it any of your business?

1. Overview

1.1 Human rights – an integral part of corporate responsibility

What do workers in a South Korean factory in South East Asia have to do with Nike's share price? How does an oil pipeline in Myanmar (Burma) land a company in court in the US? The causes of such situations are complex, but the answer, at one level, is straightforward: human rights concern business. This publication makes the business case for human rights. It provides a guide to assist managers in addressing the challenge of developing and implementing explicit human rights policies as part of their core business principles and operations.

"Companies that are good local citizens will find it easier to hire and keep talent, obtain good financing and gain societal approval, political support and regulatory consent."

Göran Lindahl, President and CEO of ABB

Human rights have become a key component of the debate on corporate responsibility. Many companies have advanced from a paternalistic, philanthropic interpretation of business in society to a broader view of the role of the corporation in society based on reputation assurance, risk management and licence to operate.

Corporate responsibility is concerned with how a company runs its core business, interacts with its business partners, and how it invests in its host communities. With increasing demand from society for accountability and transparency, with heightened vigilance by pressure groups via the Internet, and with the growing influence of ethical investors, the question of human rights is rapidly penetrating the mainstream corporate agenda. The result is that companies are having to operate within a new and evolving set of ground rules. The best starting point for companies is the existing international framework.

What are human rights?

Human rights are fundamental principles allowing the individual freedom to lead a dignified life, freedom from abuse and violations, and freedom to express independent beliefs. Human rights are based on rules of human behaviour common across diverse cultures to achieve stable, peaceful and equitable societies.

The basis of international standards of human rights is the **UN Universal Declaration of Human Rights (UDHR)** which was established in 1948 after extensive international consultation. It was adopted initially by 48 members of the UN General Assembly, and subsequently by a further 100 states. No nation has ever publicly stated its opposition to the UDHR, which is indicative of its moral weight. Its provisions have been cited as the justification for numerous United Nations actions, and have inspired or been used in many conventions and protocols adopted by the United Nations, defining in greater detail the scope and contents of international human rights standards. The two key covenants are the **International Covenant on Civil and Political Rights** (1966) and the **International Covenant on Economic, Cultural and Social Rights** (1966). These, together with **core labour standards of the International Labour Organisation** (ILO) (see Section 2.5) represent the most widely accepted codification of human rights standards as enshrined in international law.

Just an imposition of Western values?

All member countries of the UN have endorsed the UDHR. Those cultural relativists who criticise the idea of international human rights as being the product of Western imperialism or individualism ignore the wide-ranging consultation across cultures and creeds that led to the drawing up of the UDHR. They also assume a homogeneity of values within a particular culture which is highly improbable, as there is no single set of Western or Islamic or Asian cultural values. Every culture is a reservoir of themes, norms and practices which change over time. Inhumane and degrading treatment of human beings is alien to all cultures, even if it is used by some governments to serve their own political ends. States with cultures as diverse as Sweden, China, Algeria, Saudi Arabia, Australia, Kenya, and Turkey have endorsed the UDHR. An African conception of human rights, based on the UDHR, was embodied in the African Charter on Human and Peoples' Rights (1986). Different governments may or may not abide by the rights stated in the Declaration, but the fact remains that the UDHR represents a set of fundamental and universal rights over which there is a broad consensus transcending political and religious interpretation, as well as cultural identity. Not only are these applicable across a multitude of creeds and cultures, but they also offer the most widely accepted framework for promoting and protecting human rights.

Compliance with international human rights law – are companies accountable?

The UDHR calls on *'every individual and every organ of society'* to play their part in securing the observance of the rights enshrined in it. While companies may not be in the habit of referring to themselves as 'organs of society', they are a fundamental part of society. As such, they have a moral and social obligation to respect the universal rights enshrined in the Declaration. While a company is not legally obliged under international law to comply with these standards, those companies who have violated them have found, to their cost, that society at large will condemn them. A growing nucleus of transnational companies has incorporated an explicit commitment in their business principles and codes of conduct to uphold the rights enshrined in the UDHR.

The human rights architecture of the United Nations is part of international law. However, it is states, not companies, which ratify UN conventions and protocols, and which are accountable for compliance to the various monitoring bodies set up by the United Nations for this purpose. Many aspects of international human rights law are subsequently incorporated into national legislation, in which case companies become directly accountable for compliance. The European Convention on Human Rights embodies most elements of the International Covenant on Civil and Political Rights, and of the International Covenant on Social, Economic and Cultural Rights. The European Convention, which has recently been incorporated into UK law, is applied by the European Court of Human Rights in Strasbourg, whose judgements are accepted by most Western European countries.

In this way, international human rights law becomes applicable to companies by cascading down into regional and national legal systems. Even where this has not happened yet, the normative force of international human rights law is compelling companies to adopt an approach to human rights which is not based narrowly on compliance, but also on the wider values of civil society. These values are being transmitted to companies via NGOs, employees, consumers and ethically conscious shareholders.

Problems of implementation

There are major challenges facing transnational corporations (TNCs) in the implementation of human rights. Basing corporate responsibility on international human rights standards is the most effective way of ensuring comparable standards across national jurisdictions. However, the implementation of international human rights law depends on national governments through their obligations under international treaties. In reality, many TNCs will be operating in countries where the government is repressive and guilty of systematic human rights violations for political reasons. There may be other governments which are unwilling to insist on compliance with human rights standards for fear of losing foreign direct investment. TNCs can choose to hide behind governments, but in so doing, risk being judged by civil society to be complicit in violations perpetrated by the state.

On top of the problem of non-compliance with human rights standards by the host government rests the difficult question of shared responsibility between parent corporations and subsidiaries or joint venture partners. This arises particularly when TNCs attempt to distance themselves from human rights violations by claiming that they lack influence over the business practices of their subsidiaries, joint venture partners or sub-contractors. In such cases, they may be accused of complicity in the violations committed by their partners. Civil society in developed and developing countries alike is demanding more and more that TNCs actively seek to protect human rights within their legitimate sphere of influence. This sphere is perceived as extending to all business partners. Society is increasingly seeing TNCs as responsible for the human rights context of both the sourcing of their products and their end use. While there are considerable organisational challenges to companies in instituting sound human rights practices, failure to do so may result in irreparable damage to reputation.

"Getting it right is not only a matter of ethical behaviour and moral choice. Enlightened business people have realised that good business is good for business. Good business is sustainable, is part of global society, not at odds with it, and reflects values which are shared across the world."

Peter Sutherland, Chairman of BP Amoco

1.2 The business case for human rights

A company which claims a commitment to corporate responsibility cannot avoid addressing the question of human rights. Companies have a direct self-interest in using their legitimate influence to protect and promote the human rights of their employees and of the communities within which they are investing and/or operating. The increasing scrutiny of corporate behaviour by the media, consumer groups, community organisations, local and international NGOs, and the immediacy of global communication leave companies with little, if any, hiding place. Corporate reputation, licence to operate, brand image, employee recruitment and retention, share value – all these key commercial concerns are affected by society's perception of a company's behaviour with regard to human rights. This growing public awareness is focusing more and more on transnationals operating in countries where governments do not comply with internationally accepted standards of human rights.

TNCs operating in countries with repressive and corrupt governments are at particular risk of criticism from a wide array of stakeholders for complicity, tacit or active, in human rights abuses perpetrated by the state. Without an explicit human rights policy and implementation strategy which can be independently monitored and verified, companies are leaving themselves exposed to such criticisms, whether justified or not. The experience of TNCs operating in countries such as Nigeria, Colombia and Myanmar (Burma) proves that it is naïve and risky for companies not to take their human rights responsibilities very seriously.

"Stability built on repression is always false. Sooner or later the waters break the dam."

Sir John Browne,
CEO of BP Amoco

The Asian crisis of the late 1990s exposed the flawed argument that repressive governments can provide long-term political stability conducive to sustainable economic growth. The downfall of the Suharto administration in Indonesia illustrated how repression sows the seeds of social turbulence and economic crisis.

Benefits of integrating human rights into mainstream business practice

It is difficult to put figures to the business costs and benefits associated with human rights, but the connections are undeniable. Companies which are perceived as being implicated in human rights violations will see their reputation damaged, and, in some cases, their share price fall. Such companies will have problems recruiting or retaining the best employees. Their licence to operate may be threatened. Conversely, companies which can demonstrate they are actively seeking to maximise the positive impact of their operations on the human rights situation and minimise the negative impact will attract less criticism and more support from a vigilant media, networked NGOs and informed consumers, not to mention their own staff. Security costs and insurance premiums are likely to be lower in a stable environment where relations with the host community are strong than where there are serious risks of worker protests or sabotage to installations.

"The world's markets just won't buy products if they are manufactured by countries that exploit child labour, that are dictatorial, and that destroy the environment. Eventually business people will have no choice but to take part in the process of solving our social problems."

Sophon Suphaphong, President of Bangchak Petroleum
(a leading oil company in Thailand)

Benefits to business and society of integrating human rights into business practice

COMMERCIAL BENEFITS	SOCIAL BENEFITS
Enhanced corporate reputation and brand image	Strengthening the rule of law through application of international human rights standards
More secure licence to operate	
Improved employee recruitment, retention, motivation	Strengthening capacity of civil society organisations through dialogue and partnership
Diminished employee unrest, increased productivity	Encouraging other domestic and transnational companies in the sector/region to follow example of responsible business practice and corporate leadership
Improved stakeholder relations	
Reduced risk of consumer protest, boycotts, adverse publicity	
Reduced security risks and associated costs – reduced material losses, lower insurance premiums, reduced security forces	Increased trust between community groups and company through consultation and partnership activities
More sustainable relationships with business partners, sub-contractors, suppliers	Opportunity for fair representation of different community groups' views and concerns can strengthen social cohesion
Improved risk assessment and management	
Improved investment climate	
Strengthened shareholder confidence	Decline in social unrest, conflict, violent sabotage
Competitive advantage over other companies not yet adopting human rights policies	More stable employment opportunities
	Greater potential for sustainable socio-economic development

Reputation

A vital corporate asset, reputation is inextricably linked to public trust that the company will 'do the right thing'. Sir John Browne, CEO of BP Amoco, raises the issue in his introduction to BP's 1997 Social Report; *"For any company, commercial success and a highly competitive financial performance are essential. What we are learning, however, is that enduring success requires something more, and that the ability to make a constructive contribution to society and to bring positive energy to the solution of its problems is the key to the development of genuine trust and to all the opportunities which flow from that trust."*

Companies are increasingly recognising that only if they have a good reputation and social record will they be able to attract and retain the best and brightest employees. Fortune magazine and Business Week have both observed that the single most reliable predictor of overall excellence in a company is the ability to attract and retain talented employees. Recently several transnational oil company managers have observed that many of the most promising university graduate engineers are now asking questions during their job interview about the company's policy on the environment and human rights, questions which did not arise often in the past.

Reebok's experience is that the incorporation of internationally recognised human rights standards into its business practice improves worker morale and results in a higher quality working environment and higher quality products.

Excerpt from Reebok's Human Rights Production Standards

A significant proportion of the equity of many companies is tied up in the reputation of their brands, rather than in their tangible assets. This makes companies and their shareholders vulnerable to reputational damage. It is therefore not surprising that many NGOs are beginning to target companies with high profile brands, such as Nike and McDonald's. It is in this context that the London Stock Exchange is requiring companies, as a listing requirement, to have risk management systems in place to identify all major risks, including those to intangible assets such as their brand and reputation. A further requirement is that all companies make a statement on risk management in their annual reports.

Reputations Assurance: view from **PricewaterhouseCoopers**

The management of reputation integrity is one of the greatest corporate challenges of the new millennium. As forces of globalisation continue to gain momentum, society increasingly demands that large multinational corporations improve their performance in areas of human rights, the environment, worker health and safety, and other governance issues. Failure to address these demands has proved damaging to a company's most important asset – its reputation.

Glen Peters, Partner, PricewaterhouseCoopers

PricewaterhouseCoopers (PWC) has recognised that reputation is such an important asset to companies that it has developed Reputation Assurance^{SM}, a management framework and toolkit designed to help companies manage, measure, improve and report on their performance in a number of key areas of corporate responsibility. Respect for human rights is one of these. Reputation Assurance^{SM} 'provides organisations with the tools for stakeholder dialogue, performance assessment and transparency; key elements in mitigating risk, establishing trust with stakeholders, gaining a competitive advantage and preserving a company's most important asset – its reputation'. The framework has been drawn up in consultation with a variety of NGOs, including Amnesty International and Human Rights Watch. According to PWC, *"high on the corporate agenda for the 21st century will be a focus on sustainable and responsible business practices. These are not goals that can be met through a public relations campaign or vague promises of social responsibility, but must be achieved via a long-term strategic approach"*.

Benefiting the bottom line

The following observations from the Co-operative Bank illustrate how a company can benefit commercially from an ethical policy which incorporates human rights considerations.

How principles benefit the bottom line: view from the **Co-operative Bank**

The experience of the Co-operative Bank has shown that adopting an ethical approach can have positive benefits for a company, leading to long-term growth in bottom line performance. Five consecutive years of record profits is just one of several indicators of success.

The Co-operative Bank developed its ethical stance in close consultation with its customers and became the first UK clearing bank to adopt such an approach in 1992. The Bank will not do business with companies which *"oppress the human spirit, damage the environment or exploit animals"*, while at the same time it encourages organisations to adopt fair trade and ethical sourcing policies.

The ethical policy enabled the Co-operative Bank to create its own distinctive position in the very crowded financial services market where most customer propositions are based on price or service. One example of putting ethical principles into practice was the landmines campaign which the Bank adopted following the publication of the Scott Report in February 1996. The Bank placed full-page advertisements in national newspapers in order to reassure customers that their money had not been used to finance the supply of arms to both Iran and Iraq. The Bank also called on other banks to refuse to finance the manufacture and supply of landmines, which helped generate publicity around this issue.

Adopting such a high profile campaign ultimately helped to get landmines outlawed worldwide, but it also supported the Co-operative Bank's business. In addition to record profits, the Bank has benefited from unprecedented growth in customers and employee morale has improved.

Spreading ethical and environmental best practice has become an essential part of the Bank's remit. The Bank believes that its central message that 'profits and principles go hand in hand', is one that is particularly important as concern grows over economic insecurity, world-wide poverty and human rights. Business cannot ignore these wider responsibilities, as ultimately social and environmental problems will impact upon the sustainability of their operations and their capacity to generate profits.

Source: Simon Williams, Head of Corporate Affairs, The Co-operative Bank

---

"Inaction is not an option. The choice is between the exercise of corporate leadership in developing appropriate company policies, or being forced by public opinion to bring corporate practice into line with the values of society."

Sir Geoffrey Chandler, Chair of Amnesty International UK Business Group and former Shell senior executive

1.3 Integrating human rights into company operations

In recent years the well-documented policy failures of several major corporations have become salutary warnings of how human rights issues can ambush companies that are not adequately equipped to deal with them. Such cases are on the increase, exemplifying important political and social consequences of the trend towards globalisation. In particular, a decline in the power of the state, the growth of intra-state conflict, and the increasing dependency of states on transnational investment has created both threats and opportunities for companies. The existence of a vocal and well-informed international human rights community sets the stage for further reputational damage to companies that do not have sound policies in place.

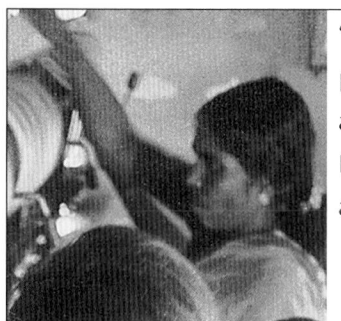

"It is a company's responsibility to anticipate and provide for human rights problems at any point in its operations in the same way that it has learnt to anticipate environmental problems. Policies need to be explicit and open. Mistakes may still be made, but secretiveness leads to the suspicion that these are at best carelessness, at worst collusion."

Pierre Sané, Amnesty International's Secretary General,
addressing a 1998 conference of the oil industry

Spheres of influence

A company's commitment to upholding international human rights standards applies in all its spheres of influence. These can be broken down broadly as follows:

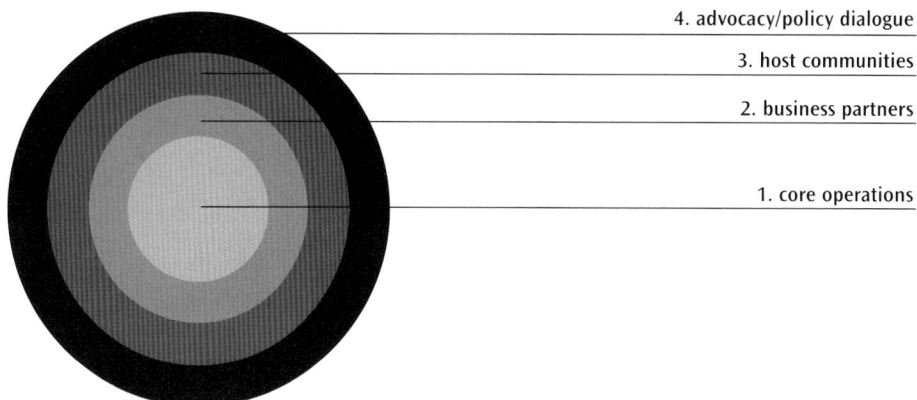

4. advocacy/policy dialogue
3. host communities
2. business partners
1. core operations

1. Core operations:

● **Labour rights:** The ILO's seven core conventions on labour standards provide the best framework for a company's human rights policy with regard to labour rights.[1] (see Section 2.5) These include guaranteeing healthy and safe working conditions, fair wages, equal pay for equal work, no forced or bonded labour, no exploitative child labour, no discrimination based on race, gender, religion, ethnic group, and the right to freedom of assembly, association and collective bargaining. A commitment to uphold these internationally recognised standards also places a responsibility on employers to defend their employees and seek legal redress in cases of arbitrary arrest, detention without fair trial, torture and extrajudicial killing. The company may choose to do this through quiet diplomacy with the government, speaking out publicly, or through the provision of legal representation for the employee.

● **Labour contracts:** employees should be made aware of their rights, with oral and written information available in their local language(s). These rights should be reflected in all employment contracts. It is important that companies facilitate worker representation as well as secure and confidential means of worker feedback to management without fear of reprisals.

● **Use of security forces:** (see Section 2.3) Companies' security procedures should be consistent with UN Basic Principles on the Use of Force and Firearms by Law Enforcement Officials and the UN Code of Conduct for Law Enforcement Officials. Companies should ensure rigorous screening and monitoring of security officials employed or contracted by the company. Clear procedures should be established by the company to deal with complaints about security personnel, including launching independent investigations and bringing cases to court where necessary.

1. ILO Convention No. 29 concerning Forced Labour; No. 87 concerning Freedom of Association and Protection of the Right to Organise; No. 98 concerning the Right to Organise and Collective Bargaining; No. 100 concerning Equal Remuneration; No. 105 concerning the Abolition of Forced Labour; No. 111 concerning Discrimination (Employment and Occupation), No. 138 concerning Minimum Age;

● **Independent monitoring, verification and reporting:** The company should set procedures for regular independent monitoring and verification of compliance with its commitment to uphold international human rights standards. This may be done by an independent NGO or NGO consortium, accredited social auditor or other independent body.

2. Business partners:
● The company needs to communicate its human rights policies and the reasons for their application to all business partners.

● The company should ensure that all contracts with joint venture partners, contractors and suppliers reflect the same commitment to human rights as the company holds.

● By agreeing from the outset mechanisms with business partners for regular independent monitoring and verification of compliance with contractual commitments to uphold international human rights standards, the company gives business partners some ownership over the process.

3. Host communities:
● The company should introduce from the outset regular consultation on questions concerning human rights. It should actively seek stakeholder engagement and partnership activities based on equity, transparency and mutual benefit.

● Stakeholder consultation is an essential element of a company's human rights impact assessment. This should form part of a company's pre-investment risk analysis, similar to an environmental impact assessment. In addition to the independent country research undertaken by Amnesty International and Human Rights Watch, there are also reports produced by the US State Department, the UK Foreign and Commonwealth Office and the Norwegian Ministry of Foreign Affairs, among others.

● By engaging in capacity-building for civil society organisations, and investing in educational and training programmes which increase community awareness of human rights issues, a company can contribute significantly to strengthening social cohesion.

4. Advocacy/dialogue with government:
● By upholding its commitment to international human rights standards in dialogue with government, a company is contributing, albeit in a small way, to a strengthening of the rule of law.

● While the influence of a TNC over a host government should not be overstated, neither should it be minimised. As a major investor and employer in a developing country, a large TNC does have considerable economic leverage with the government. Whether through quiet diplomacy with relevant government officials, public condemnation of human rights abuses, or advocacy for respect for human rights, TNCs are in a position to raise concerns about human rights abuses which adversely affect their reputation or the business environment. Specific instances of abuses that call for company intervention include arbitrary detention of labour activists, violations of human rights by state security forces deployed at a TNC installation or the unexplained disappearance of a company worker. For a TNC not to raise these concerns at the most judicious level with government officials, while adopting the argument of political neutrality or cultural relativism, is to fail to fulfil its responsibility to uphold international human rights standards. Inaction may make the company a target of labour unrest, community protest or pressure group campaigning.

"Some might question why the CEO of a multinational corporation that manufactures footwear in Indonesia, among other places, would join with human rights groups, trade unions and women's organizations to call for the release from prison of a prominent labor organizer. I did it because Ms. Dita Sari's imprisonment made it difficult for Reebok to honor our commitment to respect the human rights, including the right to organize, of the nearly 30,000 workers in Indonesia who produce our footwear. I also did it because I thought voices from the business community could make an important difference in the campaign to bring about Ms.Dita Sari's release."

Paul Fireman, chairman and CEO of Reebok International Ltd.

A corporate human rights strategy

A written commitment to the UDHR in a company's business principles is an appropriate starting point for a corporate commitment to upholding international human rights standards, but companies need to go much further. The challenge is then to implement a human rights strategy which is integrated into the mainstream business decision-making processes, with allocation of adequate resources.

Recommended considerations when drawing up a human rights strategy:

- Incorporate an explicit commitment to support the Universal Declaration of Human Rights and core ILO standards in the company's business principles and operations.

- Appoint a senior manager with responsibility for developing and mainstreaming the human rights strategy.

- Conduct wide-ranging internal and external consultation with management and employees, local and international NGOs, community groups, and other stakeholders in developing the human rights policy. This would include consultation on practical guidelines for staff on implementation and performance indicators.

- Communicate the strategy and implementation plan to all parts of the business and to all business partners. Ensure that the strategy is available in local languages.

- Conduct training for HQ and country staff to raise awareness of human rights. Include business partners in the training wherever possible. Engage relevant NGOs, human rights experts to provide input to the training.

- Conduct a human rights impact assessment as an integral part of the pre-investment risk analysis in new areas of potential operation.

- Require country managers to demonstrate their awareness of the human rights situation in their country, and of the means by which the company could proactively seek to have a positive impact on human rights. This might be through an annual letter of assurance to the Board, for example.

- Establish procedures for country managers in the event of staff being arbitrarily arrested, detained or subjected to other miscarriages of justice according to international standards

- Establish on-going dialogue with relevant NGOs or local authorities where possible on the question of improving human rights protection.

- Demonstrate a willingness to talk to critics. A defensive response attracts more criticism.

- Establish mechanisms of independent monitoring and reporting on the company's compliance with its human rights commitments.

- Act collectively with other companies to raise human rights concerns with government authorities.

Building human rights into business processes

Companies need to explore how human rights considerations can best be incorporated into existing business processes and structures. It is also important to look at what organisational change might be required to root human rights in the mainstream of the business. Human rights considerations apply from project concept through every stage in the project or product cycle to the end-user, as the diagram below indicates.

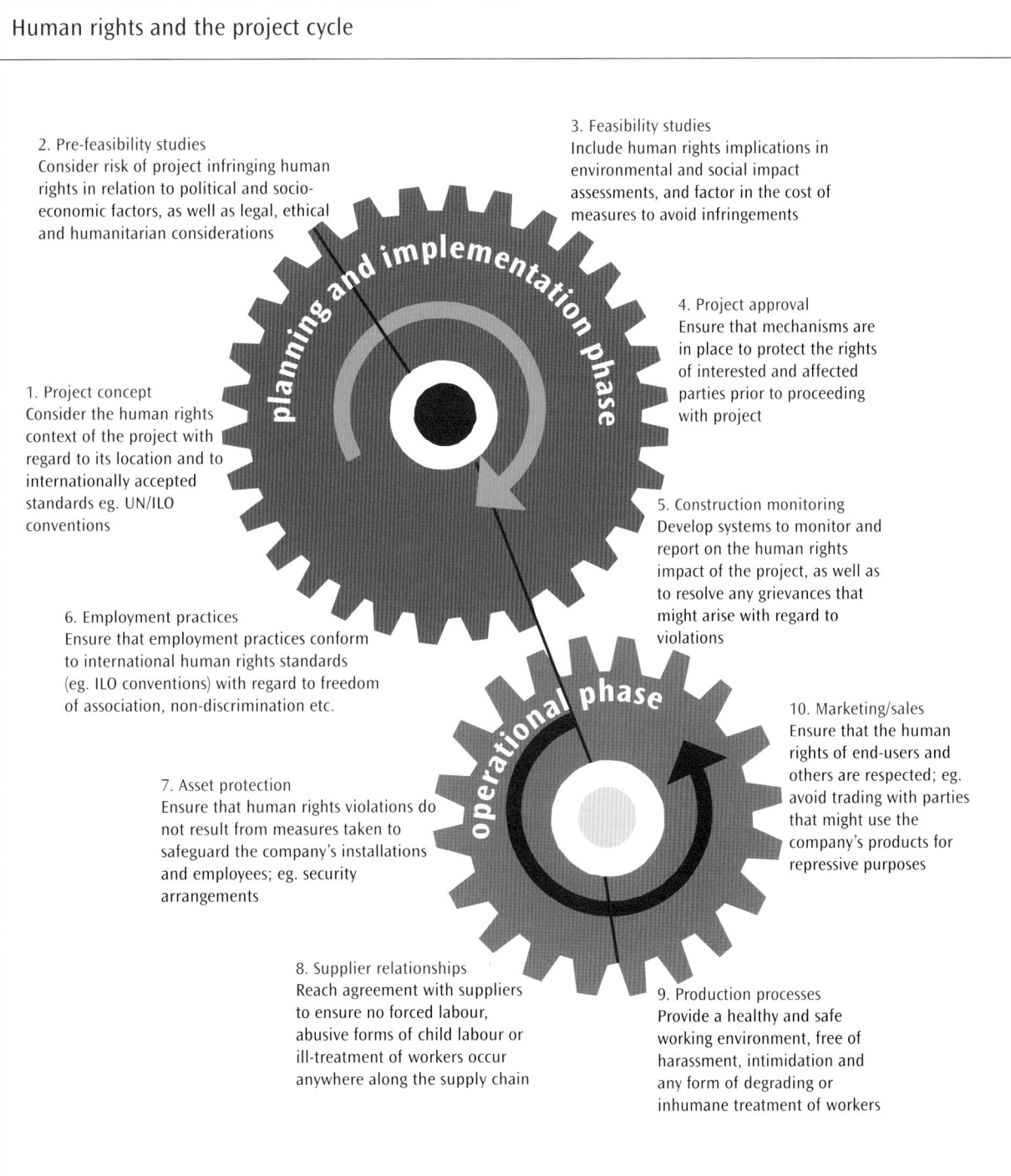

Human rights and the project cycle

2. Pre-feasibility studies
Consider risk of project infringing human rights in relation to political and socio-economic factors, as well as legal, ethical and humanitarian considerations

3. Feasibility studies
Include human rights implications in environmental and social impact assessments, and factor in the cost of measures to avoid infringements

4. Project approval
Ensure that mechanisms are in place to protect the rights of interested and affected parties prior to proceeding with project

1. Project concept
Consider the human rights context of the project with regard to its location and to internationally accepted standards eg. UN/ILO conventions

5. Construction monitoring
Develop systems to monitor and report on the human rights impact of the project, as well as to resolve any grievances that might arise with regard to violations

6. Employment practices
Ensure that employment practices conform to international human rights standards (eg. ILO conventions) with regard to freedom of association, non-discrimination etc.

10. Marketing/sales
Ensure that the human rights of end-users and others are respected; eg. avoid trading with parties that might use the company's products for repressive purposes

7. Asset protection
Ensure that human rights violations do not result from measures taken to safeguard the company's installations and employees; eg. security arrangements

8. Supplier relationships
Reach agreement with suppliers to ensure no forced labour, abusive forms of child labour or ill-treatment of workers occur anywhere along the supply chain

9. Production processes
Provide a healthy and safe working environment, free of harassment, intimidation and any form of degrading or inhumane treatment of workers

planning and implementation phase

operational phase

Organisational responsibility

The individual or team charged with responsibility for ensuring that human rights considerations are integrated throughout the business should be given access to all key centres of decision-making, from the Board downwards. Their services to the company could include the following areas:

(i) Incorporating human rights criteria into social impact assessments

An explicit requirement to assess human rights conditions within the social impact assessment process is essential. From the outset, a company needs to be identifying the potential positive and negative impacts of its proposed operations on its stakeholders, and the means by which to maximise the former and minimise the latter. Wide-ranging and ongoing consultation with local communities, NGOs and other involved parties is fundamental to this:

- assessing the impact of the proposed operation on the rights of the communities in the area – who will have access to employment opportunities generated by the company? Who will be excluded from these opportunities? Are there existing human rights problems within the communities? Are independent unions allowed? Is there any risk of forced location of communities because of the company's operations? These are just a few of the human rights questions that need to be addressed in the social impact assessment process.

- estimating potential areas of conflict between business operations and the local population's political agenda – what are the land rights of indigenous communities where the company is planning operations, are local people protesting about possible development of agricultural land?

- recommending practical and strategic ways in which the project could be improved to be more compatible with international human rights standards – which NGOs are useful to engage with, what partnership opportunities are there with local community groups, is there potential for collective action with other companies in this sector to address common problems collaboratively?

(ii) Monitoring

Two types of monitoring are important:

- *pre-emptive monitoring* with a view to anticipating and preparing for situations where the company's operations might conflict with human rights considerations

- *operational monitoring* on an ongoing basis to assess whether all the company's operations, including those run by subsidiaries and partners, have complied with the company's guidelines on human rights, and to recommend targets for improvement.

(iii) Trouble-shooting

The individual or team charged with integrating human rights into core business processes should be responsible for examining and addressing complaints about the company's conduct from human rights NGOs, minorities, indigenous groups and individuals. This will often require close coordination with other departments, such as the press and public relations departments.

Companies without a single point of responsibility for all the above areas may have problems in responding adequately to the many challenges related to human rights. Without this, responses tend to be unsatisfactory because they lack integration, making it difficult for lessons learned from past mistakes to be incorporated into future policy development.

One approach that a number of TNCs have adopted is to consolidate human rights policy into a single unit. This option makes for more consistent decision-making, and it allows the company to deal with human rights issues in a more proactive manner instead of simply responding to crises after they arise or after NGOs have drawn attention to companies' conduct. This also allows for an institutional memory to evolve which enables companies to learn more efficiently from past successes and mistakes.

Operating in a climate of human rights suppression[1]

Despite the rapid onset of globalisation, the regulatory framework for TNCs remains weak. Businesses have been left largely to themselves to work out what their obligations should be. For this reason it is crucial that human rights are built into decision-making from the outset.

For companies operating in areas of conflict or under oppressive governments, their decision-making with regard to human rights can be broken down into four areas:

● **Legal restraints and obligations,** e.g. the international standing of the government, the existence of sanctions, what international human rights covenants has the government ratified;

● **Political risks and opportunities,** e.g. political stability, factions in the conflict, perceived neutrality or partisan position of company, opportunity for dialogue with the government, risk to licence to operate;

● **Economic considerations** e.g. impact on reputation, brand, cost of security forces, risk of sabotage, extortion;

● **Ethical concerns** What are the extent, type and severity of the human rights concerns in the area? What is the company's potential/perceived role in the violations? Does having a foreign company operating in the area aggravate or ameliorate the intensity of the violations?

Companies often address the first three categories in a systematic manner, employing legal specialists, political risk analysts and business advisers to explore the relevant considerations. The fourth category, ethical concerns, has tended to be more neglected, in many cases to the cost of the companies concerned. As a result, companies have found themselves the target of high-profile campaigns by NGOs.

By simply 'doing business' with national governments which do not uphold international human rights standards, companies have unintentionally aggravated human rights disputes, particularly in cases where minority groups have claimed autonomy over an area or are in dispute over access to water, land, forestry or other resources. Even when a company's operations do not directly impact upon human rights issues, the company may nonetheless be called upon to speak out or act when an oppressive government violates its citizens' rights.

A clear human rights policy and framework for implementation will help a company navigate these challenges. This policy should be in place before entering a new country and applied on an ongoing basis. A company may invest in a country under a democratic administration which is then overthrown by a dictatorship, giving rise to a conflict situation. A strong human rights policy will help a company manage the risks caused by political instability.

1. This framework is derived from Margaret Jungk's model published in "Human Rights Standards and the Responsibility of Transnational Corporations", Kluwer Law International, 1999.

What are the options for businesses operating in a country or region where there are human rights violations?

Corporate responses

Demonstrate an active commitment to human rights	Companies are increasingly expected to demonstrate, through independent assessment and transparent reporting, what they are doing with regard to respecting and promoting human rights and how they intend to improve their performance. Partnerships with NGOs and other stakeholders help build public confidence in this regard.
Support projects to promote human rights at ground level	Many companies are already investing in the welfare of the communities within which they operate. Through supporting local community groups and NGOs, companies can contribute to a strengthening of civil society and an improved climate for human rights. Education programmes, for example, could enable citizens to become aware of their rights under international and local law and to gain the knowledge and confidence to assert these rights.
Quiet diplomacy or speaking out publicly	Silence in the face of human rights violations can be seen as tacit complicity, and a stance of neutrality is often seen as lending legitimacy to the actions of repressive governments. Companies that profess neutrality are finding it hard to maintain credibility since it is widely known that they will lobby governments vigorously when their commercial interests are at stake. Civil society is increasingly calling for companies to use their legitimate influence with governments to raise human rights concerns. ● Quiet diplomacy by company managers through appropriate government channels can prove effective in improving a situation. The willingness of some companies operating in South Africa to engage in negotiations with the government to end apartheid is a good example of this. Some companies have appealed privately to governments for the release of a particular labour activist whose detention was fuelling worker unrest. ● Under some circumstances, such as extortion and hostage-taking, it may be in a company's interests to make its concerns publicly known. NGOs and community groups will often call for the company to publicly condemn human rights violations committed by state-controlled security forces around a company's installations. This is an example of where silence would often be viewed as complicity.
Act collectively with other companies	Collectively raising concerns or negotiating with the government reduces the risk of exposure of any one company and sends a stronger message to the authorities from the international business community. A private-public-voluntary sector coalition can prove an effective force for tackling certain challenges, such as post-conflict reconstruction.

What is clear is that an increasingly vigilant NGO community and media will not ignore inaction by companies operating in a climate of human rights suppression. As Sir Geoffrey Chandler says: *"companies have a clear choice to use what influence they have, or to do nothing....If they speak out they may incur the anger of government. If silent, the certain price is reputation – which is, of course, everything."*

Framework for assessing country-specific concerns

Any company setting out to construct a set of standards for its operations in repressive states would be wise to begin by building on what has been established through the United Nations.

The UN Commission on Human Rights offers a good starting point for business. It is the principal UN body charged with receiving complaints and petitions, investigating allegations, and providing the 'evidence' for UN resolutions condemning the human rights records of governments. The Commission is served by a number of UN special rapporteurs, some of whom investigate the human rights records of designated governments, others of whom examine theme-based issues, such as freedom of religion. Their reports may be useful for a company to consider as part of its risk assessment and management processes.

Assessing country-specific concerns

How widespread are the violations?	UN special rapporteurs use clear and consistent language to convey the degree of human rights violations and the factors used in making the assessment. The assessment may range from 'sporadic, random, isolated' violations of human rights in a country to 'planned, systematic, continuous' abuse. The latter will often precipitate condemnation of the government's human rights record in the UN. The reputation of a company doing business in a country whose government's human rights record has been condemned by the UN is likely to be called into question.
Which rights are being violated?	There is much debate over the question of the cultural relativism of human rights, and the idea that certain states will emphasise different rights, according to the values of the prevailing culture. Thus Western states might give priority to civil and political rights, while Asian states might emphasise economic, cultural or social rights. However, according to the International Court of Justice, some rights are so fundamental that they are *"by their very nature"* the concern of all. These are the right to life, freedom from torture, inhumane treatment and slavery, and the right to recognition of a person before the law. The violation of such fundamental rights cannot be excused by differing cultural values, and they should be given priority in the consideration of business.
A company's connection with violations	A company operating in an area with an oppressive or unrepresentative administration may be seen to be associated with the violations. The company's connection with the violations may be perceived to be direct or indirect: ● **Direct:** where human rights violations arise directly in relation to the company's operations or products. This category includes any companies manufacturing equipment for use in the torture or suppression of dissidents; companies knowingly using child or forced labour in contravention of ILO conventions; any violation committed by company security forces while guarding company facilities or personnel – for example, troops opening fire on civilians demonstrating against the company; forcible relocation of communities to make way for company operations. ● **Indirect:** where the offending government or faction is largely supported by revenue from the company's operations, or where the company is in an industry (e.g. armaments) which enables the government to maintain its hold on power by force.

It is essential that company managers are fully aware of the human rights situation in their countries of operation, and that the risks described above are built into decision-making at all stages and levels. Country and annual reports by Amnesty International and Human Rights Watch offer valuable sources of information on the human rights situation in many countries, and companies would be wise to consult these as part of their human rights impact assessments.

2. Risks and dilemmas

Both companies and individual business people can get involved in defending those whose human rights have been violated, regardless of whether they are victims of torture, random arrests, illegal imprisonment or miscarriages of justice."

Norwegian Confederation of Business and Industry,

Human Rights Checklist for Business,1998

2. Risks and dilemmas

Many TNCs face the reality of operating in countries with repressive administrations where rule of law is weak or absent, where the independence of the judiciary is questionable, and where arbitrary arrest, detention, torture, and extrajudicial execution of activists or dissidents occur. The government may ban free trade union activity and deny its citizens the freedom of assembly and association on grounds of a threat to national security. Companies may be operating in areas of violent conflict or even civil war. Extractive or infrastructure companies may be seen by certain ethnic groups to be violating ancestral lands. The government, to whom a company is paying taxes and resource rents, may be skewing state expenditure in favour of the military and national security away from health, education and infrastructure, or in favour of one ethnic group to the detriment of others.

This primer does not provide answers to these risks and dilemmas but offers guidelines and recommendations, drawn out of concrete experience of a selection of TNCs which are tackling these issues on a daily basis in certain developing countries.

2.1 Revenue allocation and corruption

?

Are you operating in countries where corruption and lack of transparency inhibit your business?

Companies are frequently faced with problems of corruption and bribery. One issue of particular importance to the non-renewable resources sectors concerns the allocation of resource rents (royalties and taxes) on oil or minerals production. In many developing countries, the centralised nature of government is such that remote communities often derive little or no benefit from state allocated resources. This can lead to disaffection within oil or mineral producing areas, expressed through protest about or disruption of companies' operations. This in turn can lead to cycles of civil protest and government repression, as has happened in Nigeria. Companies almost inevitably risk becoming embroiled in such conflicts – while the security of personnel or assets can probably be assured, the risks to reputation may be harder to control and potentially very damaging.

Even where mechanisms exist for directing a proportion of project revenues to local development initiatives, human rights concerns can emerge. For example, the allocation of oil revenues in the Niger Delta has fuelled conflict, with inevitable implications for the oil companies operating there. BP Amoco and Occidental have been on the receiving end of allegations of complicit involvement in some cases of human rights violations in Colombia. At issue is whether the prevailing political or human rights situation presents a threat to project sustainability. For example, should projects proceed where there is little prospect for government revenues to be spent on social and human development, or where corruption and/or priority spending on armaments are the norm and human rights abuses are endemic? Dealing with these risks to project sustainability and corporate reputation is perhaps best addressed in the initial stages of project planning on the basis of established corporate policies before the commitment to develop is made.

The issue of corruption deserves particular attention. The ethical dilemmas raised by corrupt practices are of concern to many commercial organisations and the subject of The International Chamber of Commerce guidelines on 'Extortion and Bribery in International Business Transactions'. While it may be difficult at first to see the links between corruption and human rights abuses or infringements, on closer inspection pervasive corruption is clearly inimical to human rights. Firstly, in extreme cases, such as Nigeria in the 1990s, it can greatly dilute the availability of government revenues for social and economic development. Secondly, it can also lead to a loss of trust in governments and their representatives, be they elected officials or the agents of state security. In particular, where corruption pervades the activities of the police and the military, the rule of law and human rights are the inevitable victims. Where there is a loss of trust in government and its security forces, there is potential for cycles of protest and repression to develop, as described above.

Operating in such environments, TNCs face some very real ethical dilemmas and risks to their reputation by being perceived as complicit in human rights abuses. They will be judged not only by their host communities and government but also by their home parliaments, international NGOs, media and civil society organisations. In the face of these risks and dilemmas, it is simply not an option for a company to claim political neutrality. By operating in such countries, a company must face up to its responsibilities as a part of that particular society. Many companies have invested in a country under a democratic administration which is later overthrown by a dictatorship. A strong human rights policy can help reduce a company's vulnerability to sudden changes in the political climate by ensuring a consistent application of company principles.

A company should take all such issues into account in the pre-investment risk assessment and on an on-going basis during operations. Wide-ranging consultation around these issues, coupled with a strong corporate human rights strategy should help to manage these risks, and may even lead to collaborative solutions to some of the seemingly intractable problems.

2.2 Business in Conflict Zones

?

Are you operating in or considering investing in a zone of violent conflict? What is your role as a responsible company?

At the start of the 21st century, TNCs are operating in more areas prone to conflict than ever before. The commercial costs of investing in these areas are exceedingly high. Clearly, a company has a vested interest in promoting peace in areas where it is operating.

Business costs of conflict	Business benefits of peace
✗ Security costs	✓ Long-term investment potential built on healthy economies and stable societies
✗ Personnel costs	✓ Greater government spending on infrastructure & other productive purposes
✗ Reputational damage	✓ Easier access to markets, suppliers, investors, qualified employees
✗ Material losses	✓ Reduced operational costs
✗ Opportunity costs	
✗ Other risk-management costs	

"Global corporations can do more than simply endorse the virtues of the market. Their active support for better governance policies can help create environments in which both markets and human security flourish."

**UN Secretary General,
Kofi Annan, 1999**

Global market forces and the impact of business are increasingly being seen as both exacerbating conflict and having the potential to reduce conflict. Human security and social stability are critical to stable markets and growth potential. Investment by extractive and utility companies can be a factor in the dynamics of a conflict, particularly where there is dispute over access to strategic resources such as oil or water, or where conflict is occurring in the vicinity of a company's operations. In such cases, businesses cannot be neutral in their impact. Where a company is operating in a conflict zone, it has a vested interest in minimising its negative impact and maximising its positive impact on the situation, through its direct business operations, its social investment programmes and its dialogue with government, NGOs, and communities.

While there are no blueprints for the role of a company in a situation of conflict, there are steps that can be taken that will enable the company to act as a positive force for change;

Recommendations for a corporate response to operating in conflict zones

● Start from a strategic commitment from the CEO and Board to incorporate human rights considerations into business operations

● Carry out a social impact assessment which incorporates human rights criteria as part of pre-investment risk assessment

● Conduct in-house training, develop guidelines for staff operating in conflict zones

● Engage in dialogue and consultation with a range of stakeholders on a systematic and ongoing basis

● Conduct screening of security forces – follow guidelines listed in Section 2.3

● Act in partnerships with other companies, NGOs, community groups and government bodies as appropriate on projects such as community development. Collective action is often a more realistic option for a company operating in a politically sensitive environment than risking the exposure of unilateral approaches to the government.

● Implement mechanisms for evaluation and accountability through internal and independent monitoring, reporting, verification of compliance with human rights commitments, and commitments to stakeholders

● Engage in dialogue with the government, possibly with other companies and stakeholders, on issues related to conflict prevention or resolution

● Contribute to enabling frameworks for conflict prevention or resolution – working with other companies, government bodies, civil society, academia to build frameworks to address structural challenges within the conflict situation. These can include advocacy for good governance and anti-corruption measures, innovative public-private financing mechanisms for health, education, and infrastructure projects, training for local civil society organisations.

Source: "The Business of Peace", Jane Nelson, Prince of Wales Business Leaders Forum with International Alert and CEP, April 2000. This report provides extensive analysis of the role of companies in conflict situations, and offers recommendations for corporate action in pre- and post-conflict situations as well as during periods of violent conflict.

With the changing nature of conflict from cross-border to internal, from ideological to ethnically driven, from weapons of mass destruction to a proliferation of small arms, there is a growing emphasis internationally on 'multi-track diplomacy' where a number of key actors pool resources to tackle these common problems. TNCs will find that they are increasingly called upon to be one of these 'actors' in concert with other companies and stakeholders.

The following statements were made to the UK's House of Commons International Development Committee, 1998:

"Conflict threatens our whole commercial presence in a country since, for such a presence to be sustainable, we need prosperous, peaceful societies. Stability built on repression or violence is fundamentally flawed and contains the seeds of its own destruction."

BP plc

"Insecurity threatens investments in countries vulnerable to conflict, reduces the opportunities which peace could bring in future markets, and helps to make the world less stable for business dependent on trade. Investing in conflict prevention and post-conflict reconstruction is a moral imperative which also makes economic sense."

Oxfam GB

"Businesses have a strong interest in peace and security in the countries in which they are operating or might wish to operate. Conflict and instability creates risks and disruption for business in terms of heightened insecurity for staff and property, risks to investments, weakening of local markets and damage to infrastructure."

Clare Short, UK Secretary of State for International Development

The case of Angola

Angola is just one conflict-torn country where the public call for collective action is already being heard. In December 1999, the UK-based NGO Global Witness launched a campaign aimed at oil multinationals and banks investing in Angola. These included UK-based BP Amoco, French-based Elf Acquitaine (now Totalfina), US-based Exxon, Dutch-based ING Barings Bank, UK-based Lloyds TSB Bank, and Swiss-based UBS Bank. The report recommends that the oil companies form a broad coalition with the IMF, the World Bank, the international community and representatives of Angolan civil society and government to implement a policy of full transparency over state revenues. Collective action by companies is clearly more realistic where they have common values and principles. If companies each have a commitment to upholding the principles of the UDHR, this provides a starting point for collaboration. The unfortunate reality is that very few companies as yet share this commitment.

Oil and diamonds fuel war in Angola

The renewed conflict in Angola since the late 1990s and the accompanying human rights abuses and violations of laws of war have been fuelled by new flows of arms into the country. This has occurred despite the UN arms embargo on the armed opposition, UNITA, which has been in place since 1993. UNITA financed the rebuilding of its military through its control of Angola's diamond wealth.

The Angolan government received arms shipments throughout the Lusaka peace process. Although this was not illegal, it undermined the spirit of the Lusaka Protocol and contributed to a lack of confidence in the peace process. The government has paid for its arms purchases largely through $870 million of funds generated in 1999 from signature bonus payments on oil exploration, of which BP-Amoco, Exxon and Elf Aquitaine were the main contributors.

According to the Angolan foreign minister, these funds were earmarked for the *"war effort."*

Lack of conditionality

There appear to be no conditionalities tied to these large signature bonus payments, meaning that the government of Angola can spend these funds on whatever weapons systems it desires, including ones that are highly indiscriminate such as antipersonnel landmines and cluster bombs. At the very least, international oil companies should encourage the government to reach a "shadow agreement" – an audit that ensures that all future oil profit remittances are spent in a transparent manner and not for covert arms purchases, in particular not for the purchase of indiscriminate weapons. Oil companies should also assist the UN's sanctions committee to locate the source of UNITA fuel. They can ensure that their affiliates in Angola's neighbouring states are aware of the oil and petroleum embargo on UNITA and are required to inform the national police and the UN of

any suspicious bulk purchasing of fuel so that fuel does not reach UNITA.

Breaches of embargo

International diamond companies and dealers also have responsibilities. They should refuse to purchase or distribute any diamonds suspected of having been acquired in violation of the UN embargo and inform the police and the UN of the source of such diamonds. They should assist in the implementation of a global monitoring and certification scheme to ensure compliance with the UN embargo. Since there is some disagreement over identification of Angolan rough diamonds, they should also assist the UN in developing criteria and means to establish the origin of these.

The nub of the problem is that human rights protection has not attracted much interest from the large transnational oil and diamond companies that extract the majority of Angola's wealth. While some of the companies are aware of how costly it can be to their reputation to come into the spotlight for being implicated in human rights violations, the measures they are taking to prevent this happening are minimal.

Source: *Angola Unravels: The Rise and Fall of the Lusaka Peace Process,* **Human Rights Watch, September 1999**

Lord Avebury and BP Amoco Chairman Peter Sutherland exchange views (1999)

Dear Mr Sutherland

I read your paper on The Role of the Business Sector in the Development and Protection of Human Rights, published by Amnesty International, with interest, and I agree with you in your conclusion that the business sector can be a fundamental force for good.

I hope you would also agree with me that business can also, indirectly and unintentionally, cause harm.

According to Africa Confidential the Angolan government is hoping to raise more than US$800 million in signature bonuses from the operating companies and their equity partners in certain deep water blocks, and to use the proceeds to fund the civil war, including arms procurement. Luanda is reported to have already appointed the leading operator in each block: BP-Amoco (26.6 per cent in Block 31); Elf-Aquitaine (30 per cent in Block 32), and Exxon (35 per cent in Block 33). The final agreements, and the handing over of signature bonus cash, are reported to be held up as the government chooses the remaining equity partners in each block. The interest of both oil and arms traders is said to focus on three companies – Pro-Dev, Falcon and Naphta – which have links to defence and security specialists but little apparent expertise in upstream oil production.

If this report is correct, the signature money you and others will pay the Angolan Government is not to be used for development but to ratchet up the civil war that has already caused an enormous amount of misery and loss of life. We can all agree that Savimbi is the main culprit, but can there be a purely military solution to Angola's tragedy?

Yours sincerely

E. Avebury

BP Amoco

Dear Lord Avebury.

Thank you very much for your letter of 18 May, and your kind remarks about my speech. I should like to say at the outset that I recognise the legitimacy and force of your arguments, and I acknowledge that you are raising difficult issues...

You raise the specific issue of signature bonuses. We have no means of ensuring that these are not used to help finance the Government's war effort. Not everyone would agree that global companies have the right or legitimacy to tell lawful governments what they should, or should not, spend their money on. What we will do is to insist as far as we can that such payments are transparent. Governments can be challenged by their electorates and public opinion generally to justify where the money has been spent. Moreover, the payment of signature bonuses in the oil industry is standard practice (including even in the United States of America) and the payments made in Angola are both on a per barrel and per square kilometre basis comparable with the Gulf of Mexico. It would be very difficult to refuse Angola what is standard practice elsewhere, and of course often we are accused of paying too little...

Our experience elsewhere – and particularly in South Africa – leads us to believe that we are capable of being a force for the good, provided we behave in a way which is consistent with our stated business policies...

Yours sincerely.

Peter Sutherland

The map illustrates the exposure of a number of major UK companies in countries where human rights violations are prevalent.

A geography of corporate risk: UK transnational companies

KEY

Violation Type

1. Torture
2. 'Disappearances'
3. Extra-judicial executions
4. Hostage-taking
5. Harassment of human rights defenders
6. Denial of freedom of association
7. Forced labour
8. Bonded labour
9. Forcible relocation
10. Systematic denial of women's rights
11. Prisoners of conscience

Source: Amnesty International (1999)

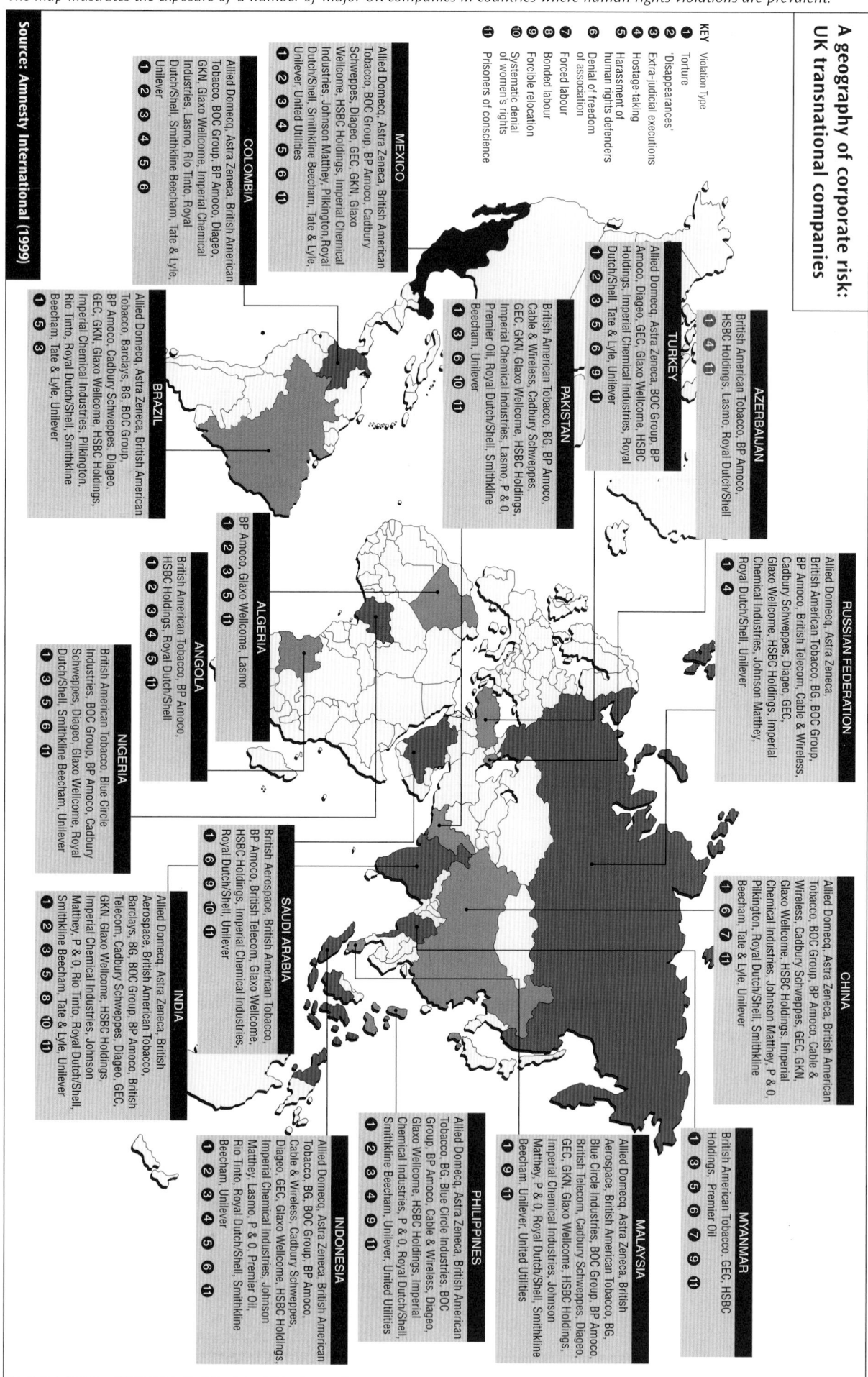

MEXICO
Allied Domecq, Astra Zeneca, British American Tobacco, BOC Group, BP Amoco, Diageo, Schweppes, Diageo, GEC, GKN, Glaxo Wellcome, HSBC Holdings, Imperial Chemical Industries, Lasmo, Rio Tinto, Royal Dutch/Shell, SmithKline Beecham, Tate & Lyle, Unilever, United Utilities
1 2 3 4 5 6

COLOMBIA
Allied Domecq, Astra Zeneca, British American Tobacco, BOC Group, BP Amoco, Diageo, GKN, Glaxo Wellcome, Imperial Chemical Industries, Johnson Matthey, Pilkington, Royal Dutch/Shell, SmithKline Beecham, Tate & Lyle, Unilever
1 2 3 4 5 6 6

BRAZIL
Allied Domecq, Astra Zeneca, British American Tobacco, Barclays, BG, BOC Group, BP Amoco, Cadbury Schweppes, Diageo, GEC, GKN, Glaxo Wellcome, HSBC Holdings, Imperial Chemical Industries, Pilkington, Rio Tinto, Royal Dutch/Shell, SmithKline Beecham, Tate & Lyle, Unilever
1 5 3

TURKEY
Allied Domecq, Astra Zeneca, BOC Group, BP Amoco, Diageo, GEC, Glaxo Wellcome, HSBC Holdings, Imperial Chemical Industries, Royal Dutch/Shell, Tate & Lyle, Unilever
1 2 3 6 9 11

AZERBAIJAN
British American Tobacco, BP Amoco, HSBC Holdings, Lasmo, Royal Dutch/Shell
1 4 11

PAKISTAN
British American Tobacco, BG, BP Amoco, Cable & Wireless Cadbury Schweppes, GEC, GKN, Glaxo Wellcome, HSBC Holdings, Imperial Chemical Industries, Lasmo, P & O, Premier Oil, Royal Dutch/Shell, SmithKline Beecham, Unilever
1 3 6 10 11

ALGERIA
BP Amoco, Glaxo Wellcome, Lasmo
1 2 3 5 11

ANGOLA
British American Tobacco, BP Amoco, HSBC Holdings, Royal Dutch/Shell
1 2 3 4 5 11

NIGERIA
British American Tobacco, Blue Circle Industries, BOC Group, BP Amoco, Cadbury Schweppes, Diageo, Glaxo Wellcome, Royal Dutch/Shell, SmithKline Beecham, Unilever
1 3 5 6 11

SAUDI ARABIA
British Aerospace, British American Tobacco, BP Amoco, British Telecom, Glaxo Wellcome, HSBC Holdings, Imperial Chemical Industries, Royal Dutch/Shell, Unilever
1 6 9 10 11

INDIA
Allied Domecq, Astra Zeneca, British Aerospace, British American Tobacco, Barclays, BG, BOC Group, BP Amoco, British Telecom, Cadbury Schweppes, Diageo, GEC, GKN, Glaxo Wellcome, HSBC Holdings, Imperial Chemical Industries, Johnson Matthey, P & O, Rio Tinto, Royal Dutch/Shell, SmithKline Beecham, Unilever
1 2 3 4 5 6 11

INDONESIA
Allied Domecq, Astra Zeneca, British American Tobacco, BG, BOC Group, BP Amoco, Cable & Wireless, Cadbury Schweppes, Diageo, GEC, Glaxo Wellcome, HSBC Holdings, Imperial Chemical Industries, Johnson Matthey, Lasmo, P & O, Premier Oil, Rio Tinto, Royal Dutch/Shell, SmithKline Beecham, Unilever
1 2 3 4 5 6 11

PHILIPPINES
Allied Domecq, Astra Zeneca, British American Tobacco, BG, BOC Group, BP Amoco, British Telecom, Cadbury Schweppes, Diageo, GEC, GKN, Glaxo Wellcome, HSBC Holdings, Imperial Chemical Industries, P & O, Royal Dutch/Shell, SmithKline Beecham, Unilever, United Utilities
1 2 3 4 9 11

MALAYSIA
Allied Domecq, Astra Zeneca, British Aerospace, British American Tobacco, BG, Blue Circle Industries, BOC Group, BP Amoco, British Telecom, Cadbury Schweppes, Diageo, GEC, GKN, Glaxo Wellcome, HSBC Holdings, Imperial Chemical Industries, Johnson Matthey, P & O, Royal Dutch/Shell, SmithKline Beecham, Unilever, United Utilities
1 9 11

MYANMAR
British American Tobacco, GEC, HSBC Holdings, Premier Oil
1 3 5 6 7 9 11

CHINA
Allied Domecq, Astra Zeneca, British American Tobacco, BOC Group, BP Amoco, Cable & Wireless, Cadbury Schweppes, GEC, GKN, Glaxo Wellcome, HSBC Holdings, Imperial Chemical Industries, Johnson Matthey, P & O, Royal Dutch/Shell, SmithKline Beecham, Tate & Lyle, Unilever
1 6 7 11

RUSSIAN FEDERATION
Allied Domecq, Astra Zeneca, British American Tobacco, BG, BOC Group, BP Amoco, British Telecom, Cable & Wireless, Cadbury Schweppes, Diageo, GEC, Glaxo Wellcome, HSBC Holdings, Imperial Chemical Industries, Johnson Matthey, Royal Dutch/Shell, Unilever
1 4

Above data derived from 1998 Company Accounts (listings under Principal subsidiaries, associates and joint ventures, other notes on investments and reference in the main text of the report) and/or company web site. The data was verified by all the companies concerned, with the exceptions of P & O and SmithKline Beecham which did not respond to Amnesty International UK's request. The human rights violations associated with each country are not a comprehensive list, but have been selected from Amnesty International sources because of their relevance to corporate risk.

2.3 Security forces

Are there any state or private security forces deployed at any of your installations? What are the associated risks of human rights infringements? How can these be minimised?

The UN Development Programme's Human Development report of 1999 claims that 'defence is becoming privatised and international private military firms are proliferating. In some countries, mercenaries sell their services for mining and energy concessions…And more and more, the clients of these mercenaries are multinational corporations seeking to protect their mining interests in conflict-prone countries.'

Violence and instability in a number of countries today make it necessary for companies to defend their personnel and property by using their own armed guards or by entering into arrangements with private security firms or with state security forces. These arrangements can be among the most dangerous in terms of human rights violations and harm to companies' reputations.

Wherever security forces are needed, companies need to be addressing a number of questions from the pre-investment phase onwards. Who is responsible for providing the security services to the company? What are the contractual arrangements with the security forces? Is it possible to screen privately contracted security guards for past human rights violations? What procedures does the company have in place if security forces, who are guarding its installations, commit violations against local protestors?

Key considerations for companies using state or private security forces:

Security is an issue for companies across several sectors, but is perhaps of particular relevance to the extractive sector. Oil, gas and mining companies have, to date, experienced the most challenging problems with security forces deployed at their installations.

- In situations where the presence of government and the rule of law are weak, and where social and economic development are poor, companies can find themselves becoming the target of peoples' frustrations with the perceived failures of government (as the only local organisation with any link, however tenuous, to government). In such situations, company employees or contractors may be at risk from hostage-taking or other forms of revenue-seeking behaviour.

- If the communities most affected by the adverse consequences of resource development do not perceive themselves as net beneficiaries from such developments, protests will almost inevitably emerge. Where such protests are likely to be met with repression and human rights infringements (and possibly military intervention), the companies concerned are at risk of being implicated in abuses of human rights.

- The true value of mineral or oil resources is inextricably linked to the ability to extract securely, process and export such materials. Where the intervention of military forces is deemed necessary to provide assurances of security, such as in situations of internal conflict, the risks to companies from becoming complicitly linked to human rights abuses is considerable.

- At the strategic planning stage, companies should consider the security implications of developing oil or mineral resources. For example, the case study on the Australian-based minerals development company, WMC Resources, illustrates the company's policy commitment not to invest in situations where the military will be required to provide security as this would prevent it from obtaining a licence to operate from local communities.

- Companies should maximise their efforts to rely on passive and preventative security measures that pose minimal risks to the human rights of the local population. Companies should seek to underpin such measures through engaging with communities in a proactive manner, to gain their consent and help ensure that they perceive themselves as net beneficiaries. In this way the company is most likely to obtain its licence to operate.

Below are specific guidelines for companies for their dealings with security forces, which were drawn up by Human Rights Watch and have been endorsed by Amnesty International UK.

Human Rights Watch – specific recommendations to companies on security arrangements

- Companies should insert a clause into any security agreement signed with the government or any state entity that requires, as a condition of contract, that state security forces operating in the area of company installations conform to the human rights obligations the government has assumed under the International Covenant on Civil and Political Rights and other international human rights norms.

- Companies' security agreements with state entities should be made public with the sole exception of operational details that could jeopardise individuals' lives.

- Companies should screen the military and police who are assigned for their protection. They should seek to ensure that no soldier or police agent credibly implicated in human rights abuse be engaged in their protection.

- Careful background checks should be undertaken to ensure that former police or military officers who work as private contractors or as part of company security staff have no history of human rights abuses or paramilitary involvement.

- Companies must make absolutely clear to the police and military defending them – as well as to company staff and sub-contracted personnel – that human rights violations will not be tolerated, and that companies will be the first to press for investigation and prosecution if any abuses occur.

- Whenever credible allegations of human rights abuses surface, companies should insist that any soldiers and officers implicated be immediately suspended and the appropriate internal and criminal investigations launched.

- Companies should actively monitor the status of the investigations and press for resolution of the cases. If the investigations or prosecutions are stalled, companies should publicly condemn the failure to conduct or complete the investigations.

- Any material assistance given by companies to security forces must be non-lethal and subject to external auditing.

Source: Arvind Ganesan, Human Rights Watch, Washington DC, US

The experiences of Shell in Nigeria demonstrate how and why security considerations have become a key factor in the transformation of the company's approach to human rights. This is illustrated in the following summary. The full case study is in Part II.

Shell – Linking security to human rights in Nigeria

Prompted in part by public reaction to allegations of complicity in human rights violations in Nigeria, Shell began to engage with a range of stakeholders and NGOs in 1996, including Amnesty International and Human Rights Watch, regarding the security aspects of their Nigerian operations. This led to a revision of Shell's rules of engagement with the state security forces – the police and the military – to accommodate the *UN Basic Principles on the Use of Force and Firearms* and the *UN Code of Conduct for Law Enforcement Officials*. The experience in Nigeria has prompted a broader-based review of security provision and the development and adoption in 1998 of group-wide *Use of Force Guidelines*. These provide for, *inter alia*, seeking assurances from state forces that the use of force will respect human dignity and people's rights, will be proportional to the threat, will minimise damage and injury, and advising them that they will be held accountable for any excessive use of force.

All Shell security personnel are to receive adequate training in operating procedures that are consistent with relevant codes of conduct. The guidelines stipulate the 'rules of engagement' for calling in or contracting with state security forces. They also provide advice on acceptable courses of action and responses against those who represent a threat to the security or safety of personnel or company assets.

In Nigeria, Shell have a legal obligation to call in the forces of law and order in situations where people or property are at risk, yet they have publicly committed themselves to not hiding behind a military shield. The emphasis is on passive preventative security, which avoids the need to use force. The *Use of Force Guidelines* and associated procedures feature in the training Shell provides to the Nigerian Police detachment assigned to protecting the company's assets. Shell reserves the right to screen and reject police based on their possible involvement in human rights abuses. Their current rules of engagement are discussed with other state security forces in their areas of operation, as are the conditions under which security forces will be called in.

In recent years, Shell has become more active in its efforts to promote human rights in the Delta. For example, after the arrest of Batom Mittee and others during the January 1998 Ogoni day celebrations, Shell appealed for the highest standards of human rights to be upheld. Shell also lobbied the government for the withdrawal of the Mobile Police from Ogoni land in the interests of creating an atmosphere conducive to reconciliation. Batom Mittee was subsequently released and the Mobile Police withdrawn.

There is an emerging consensus that for peace and stability to be restored to the Niger Delta, the communities must view themselves as net beneficiaries from oil production. Achieving that shift in perspective is no easy task, given the legacy of past failures by governments, persecution by security forces, inter-ethnic rivalries, and the sense that oil companies have put profits before principles. Shell believes that it has a contribution to make towards helping change perceptions. This includes a responsibility to continue to demonstrate support for human rights. Whether or not communities finally come to see themselves as beneficiaries depends not only on Shell, but also crucially on the Nigerian government and on the ethnic groups living in the Delta.

Source: Robin Aram, Vice President of External Relations and Policy Development, Shell International

2.4 Land rights and indigenous peoples' rights

?

Do your company's operations impinge on indigenous communities?
Are their land rights under threat?

Why are indigenous peoples' rights an issue for companies?

Significant attention is being given to indigenous issues by governments, public interest organisations and pressure groups. The growth of oil and gas exploration and production and mining in remote regions has given rise to demands that companies take account of indigenous claims to land and resources as an integral part of the project planning process. Violent conflicts have occurred in the past, causing immense damage to the prestige of energy and mining companies.

The indigenous issue pervades far more than isolated regions of so-called "developing countries". It is a major political issue is some industrialised countries, in such places as Alaska, Australia, Canada, Russia and parts of Scandinavia. The past few years in particular have seen complex negotiations over land and treaty rights, control over mineral development, profit-sharing and compensation arrangements. A significant number of countries have seen fit to amend their laws and policies on indigenous issues while new declarations, conventions, policy guidelines of multilateral financial institutions, and proposed codes of conduct for corporations present new operational challenges for companies.

When considering corporate responsibility towards indigenous peoples, at issue is the reality that these communities usually have a critical dependence on the land. They tend not to work in the formal sector, their literacy rates may be low, and they are least likely to benefit from the employment opportunities provided by private sector investment. At the same time, they are often most vulnerable to the negative consequences of this investment, such as forced relocation, and are the least well placed to pursue legal compensation for loss of livelihoods.

Shell's primer on business and indigenous peoples[1] indicates that the company is actively seeking to raise awareness of these issues amongst its staff. This is a welcome and progressive step by a leading TNC. A number of other TNCs have adopted policies on indigenous peoples in recent years. The challenge lies in the implementation of these policies.

Respect for the aspirations and demands of indigenous peoples worldwide can provide positive benefits for companies as well as for society at large. Indigenous communities can have strong ideas about the management of their local resources, both renewable and non-renewable, and can be valuable partners if constructively engaged. A responsible approach to this issue can reap dividends in terms of reputation, good community relations and the smooth operation of a project. As always, the framework of internationally accepted standards on the rights of tribal and indigenous peoples is the best starting point for companies.

1. under preparation at time of going to print, April 2000

International standards and guidelines

Definitions

The ILO standards distinguish between 'indigenous' and 'tribal' peoples, while according them the same rights. Tribal peoples are defined through distinct lifestyles, indigenous through a combination of descent and the retention of distinct institutions. The UN Draft Declaration on Indigenous Rights currently avoids a precise definition. The World Bank's working definition emphasises vulnerability, and functional criteria including attachment to ancestral territories, a different language, and primarily subsistence production. All texts stress the importance of "self-definition" by indigenous peoples and stress the need to identify indigenous lands, to guarantee effective protection of land rights, to safeguard against forced relocation, and to punish unauthorised intrusion.

Land rights – the legal framework

There are at present two ILO Conventions, No.107 on **Indigenous and Tribal Populations** (1957) and No. 169 on **Indigenous and Tribal Peoples** (1989), which pertain directly to indigenous peoples. Convention No. 169 contains seven articles on indigenous land and resource rights, in the latter area creating new provisions of international law. It includes the following key articles:

- Governments are required to take the necessary steps to identify the lands which indigenous peoples traditionally occupy, to guarantee their effective protection, and to establish legal procedures to deal with indigenous land claims
- Indigenous rights to the natural resources pertaining to their lands shall be specially safeguarded. In cases where the State retains the ownership of mineral or sub-surface resources or other resource rights pertaining to lands, governments should maintain consultation procedures to ascertain whether and to what degree indigenous interests would be prejudiced, before undertaking or permitting any programmes for resource exploration or exploitation.
- Indigenous peoples should wherever possible participate in the benefits of such activities and receive fair compensation for any damages sustained.

In addition, the UN has a Draft Declaration of Indigenous Rights, which, it is hoped, will lead to a UN Convention on this issue. These instruments provide a good starting point for companies seeking to avoid infringements of indigenous rights. The standards stress the special importance of lands and territories for the cultures and spiritual values of indigenous peoples, as well as the collective aspects of this relationship. They aim to establish the strongest possible rights for indigenous peoples over lands, territories and the total environment, and to avoid forced relocation to whatever extent possible.

Resource rights and profit sharing

These international standards aim to secure special safeguards for indigenous peoples, concerning rights to natural resources pertaining to their lands. The ILO Convention 169 stresses consultative procedures before mineral exploration and exploitation, participation "wherever possible" in the benefits, and fair compensation for damages. The UN Draft Declaration stresses the right to free and informed indigenous consent prior to any project authorisation. It has been World Bank policy for some time to make its support for mineral and hydro-carbon projects conditional on indigenous participation in the benefits and compensation for damages where indigenous peoples' rights are adversely affected.

Source: International Labour Organisation

Avoiding infringements

Dispute over access to land and land rights has historically led to serious infringements of citizens' civil and political rights. Protests over land use have often resulted in intervention by military or police forces, and arrest and detention of protesters, even where such protests were peaceful and within the law. Governments are usually anxious to minimise these disturbances for fear of disinvestment by companies.

While international human rights instruments provide companies with the parameters within which to develop a policy addressing indigenous rights, the problems facing a company will vary depending on local circumstances. In a place such as the Indonesian outer islands, where the institutional framework for indigenous rights is almost non-existent, it may be difficult to identify any local or national organisation with which to consult. In Latin America, on the other hand, there are increasingly sophisticated organisations representing indigenous organisations at all levels and some legal instruments for them to use. The difficulty for many companies is how to reach agreement on revenue-sharing and compensation when there is no legal framework on which to draw. An additional complication arises in joint ventures with state-owned companies.

Key considerations for companies regarding land rights and indigenous peoples' rights:

- Some of the defining characteristics of indigenous peoples include their close attachment to ancestral territories, unique languages and dependency on subsistence agriculture. Irrespective of the geographic context, developing an understanding of indigenous peoples' perspectives and way of life is the starting point for respecting their human rights.

- In many situations, indigenous peoples do not enjoy security of tenure. In such situations, the potential for infringement of the rights of indigenous peoples is high. Resource development companies would do well to develop an understanding about land tenure in the vicinity of their operations, and of the threats to ancestral lands. This should be factored into development decision-making.

- Irrespective of whether companies are legally obliged to ensure the free and informed consent of indigenous peoples to proceed with developments on their ancestral lands, they should strive to achieve free and informed consent. While this may involve a high degree of consultation and community participation, the longer-term benefits to projects are worthwhile.

This also applies to other situations (such as remote areas) where communities may be particularly vulnerable to the adverse consequences of large-scale developments.

- In dealing with indigenous peoples, companies should be aware of the wealth of traditional knowledge that such communities may have that may be relevant to project decision-making. They should also look to develop mutual understanding with indigenous peoples as the basis for helping to protect their rights through participatory decision-making.

The experiences of the Australian mineral company, WMC Resources in the Philippines, may provide some useful insights into handling the issue of land rights and indigenous people's rights. These are summarised below. The full case study is in Part II.

WMC Resources – Learning to respect indigenous land rights

The experience of WMC Resources, the Australian-based minerals company, at Tampakaen in the Philippines provides some valuable insights into how companies can avoid a 'clash of cultures' and develop relationships of mutual respect with indigenous peoples.

The focus of WMC's exploration activities is home to some 2,300 people belonging to five indigenous Bla'an communities which have traditionally engaged in hunting and slash and burn agriculture, practices that are still prevalent.

The history of the Bla'an interaction with logging companies is one punctuated by broken promises. Some Bla'an formed armed groups to combat the military, and their successful resistance led to an amnesty being issued for the Bla'an during the Aquino Presidency. WMC have had to contend with the Bla'an deep-seated mistrust of outsiders – the legacy of progressive encroachment by settlers and logging companies.

Under the terms of its Financial and Technical Assistance Agreement with the Philippine Government, WMC is obliged to "recognise and respect the rights, customs and traditions of indigenous tribal peoples". This is broadly consistent with the Indigenous Peoples Policy that WMC adopted in 1995— the first policy produced by a mining company that committed itself to developing relationships of mutual understanding and respect with indigenous peoples.

Consultations with tribal leaders during the early stages of exploration highlighted the protection of traditional lands and securing legal title as the primary concerns of the Bla'an.

WMC and the five indigenous Bla'an communities in the proposed minerals development area signed 'Heads of Agreement' in 1994 and 1995, in which the company committed itself to supporting their ancestral domain claims. Over the next two years, detailed ethnographic and archaeological records were prepared and the boundaries of traditional territories were mapped. Reports compiling the work in support of the ancestral domain claims were submitted to the Government by four of the five Bla'an communities. To date, four have been awarded Certificates of Ancestral Domain, which recognise their rights to occupy and use the land.

Elsewhere in the Philippines, it is common practice for the military to secure access to lands on behalf of companies. WMC claims that it has consistently resisted any military involvement in obtaining such access or security provision at Tampakaen. Its policy has been that it would be unable to obtain the support of communities or achieve its business objectives by relying on a military force to provide security. The relatively low-key security presence around its facilities indicates that WMC may be having some success in gaining the confidence of local communities, and that, on balance, it may be on the path to earning a local licence to operate.

At Tampakaen, WMC has helped indigenous communities to secure Certificates of Ancestral Domain Claim which they might not otherwise have obtained in a fairly short time-frame. They have attempted to develop a relationship of mutual benefit with indigenous communities and to ensure that lasting community benefits remain, even if the project does not proceed. They have also respected the choice of one Bla'an community to deny them access to their lands. Finally, they have taken steps to develop an informed understanding amongst communities of the implications of mining.

Whether these steps are merely an attempt by the company to buy legitimacy, and thereby gain their licence to operate from the Philippines Government, or whether they represent a genuine attempt to involve and empower the communities that will be affected, will only emerge if the project is ultimately developed.

Source: Gavan Collery, Manager of Corporate Affairs, WMC Resources Ltd.

2.5 Labour rights

This section does not provide an exhaustive list of labour rights, but instead highlights those where companies have come up against problems most frequently. It lays out the principles as defined in international standards, recommends concrete action by companies to uphold these principles, and draws key lessons from company case studies relating to a particular labour right. The full company case studies which elaborate on these labour rights issues in Part II illustrate aspects of good practice which may be of use to other companies in addressing similar challenges.

Positive steps that companies can take to protect labour rights

The most appropriate starting point for companies are the seven ILO core conventions, which have the status of international law. ILO conventions, once ratified, create binding obligations on governments. Even in the absence of ratification, they serve as a standard of reference for national law and practice. Companies should have explicit policies and procedures in place to ensure that they do not violate any of these conventions. In addition, companies should determine how they can use their legitimate influence over government, police, security forces and other agencies to protect the human rights of their own employees and of all workers that form part of their supply chain.

Key ILO Conventions

No. 29	Forced Labour Convention (1930): Requires the suppression of forced or compulsory labour in all its forms. Certain exceptions are permitted, such as military service, convict labour properly supervised, emergencies such as wars, fires, earthquakes.
No. 87	Freedom of Association and Protection of the Right to Organise Convention (1948): Establishes the right of all workers and employers to form and join organisations of their own choosing without prior authorisation, and lays down a series of guarantees for the free functioning of organisations without interference by public authorities.
No. 98	Right to Organise and Collective Bargaining Convention (1949): Provides for protection against anti-union discrimination, for protection of workers' and employers' organisations against acts of interference by each other, and for measures to promote collective bargaining.
No. 100	Equal Remuneration Convention (1951): Calls for equal pay and benefits for men and women for work of equal value.
No. 105	Abolition of Forced Labour Convention (1957): Prohibits the use of any form of forced or compulsory labour as a means of political coercion or education, punishment for the expression of political or ideological views, workforce mobilisation, labour discipline, punishment for participation in strikes, or discrimination.
No. 111	Discrimination (Employment and Occupation) Convention (1958): Calls for a national policy to eliminate discrimination in access to employment, training and working conditions, on grounds of race, colour, sex, religion, political opinion, national extraction or social origin and to promote equality of opportunity and treatment.
No. 138	Minimum Age Convention (1973): Aims at the abolition of child labour, stipulating that the minimum age for employment shall not be less than the age of completion of compulsory schooling.

Freedom of association and the right to collective bargaining

?

Do all employees of your company and of your business partners have the right to join free trade unions? If not, how are workers' interests represented?

The international standards

Freedom of association is a core right enshrined in the UDHR and two ILO core conventions. ILO Convention No. 87, on the Freedom of Association and Protection of the Right to Organise, establishes the right of all workers and employers to form and join organisations of their own choosing without prior authorisation, and lays down a set of guarantees for the free functioning of organisations without interference by the public authorities. ILO Convention No. 89 on the Right to Organise and Collective Bargaining provides for protection against anti-union discrimination, for protection of workers' and employers' organisations against acts of interference by each other, and for measures to promote collective bargaining.

The debate

The most fought-over of international labour standards are the rights to associate and engage in collective bargaining. These are considered core 'enabling rights' without which workers and owners cannot negotiate fair agreements which make sense in the local context. Many in the business community and in governments in the developed and developing world have sought to find ways around these rights in order to prevent unions finding an opening from which to organise. Some businesses and governments accuse unions of being undemocratic, self-interested, and a threat to corporate and national competitiveness. Unions counter that these criticisms reflect at best an unwillingness to allow workers a fair chance to negotiate fair conditions, and at worst the views of corrupt and dictatorial business and government leaders interested in keeping labour costs down and denying workers a voice.

While the debate continues, unionists and labour activists in many countries are still being harassed or persecuted for their actions. In 1998 alone, the International Confederation of Free Trade Unions (ICFTU) estimates that 2,000 union activists were assassinated or tortured. It is a challenge but not an insurmountable obstacle facing companies operating in countries such as China and Vietnam, where free trade union activity is not permitted by the state, to seek legal means to uphold their commitment to protecting core labour rights.

Recommendations for building the right to freedom of association and the right to collective bargaining into a company's labour practices:

● Base company principles on ILO Convention No. 87 on the Freedom of Association and Protection of the Right to Organise, and No. 89 on the Right to Organise and Collective Bargaining.

● Incorporate company principles into all contracts with joint venture partners and sub-contractors, and build these principles into monitoring of business partners' practices.

● Ensure workers are aware of their rights through making company principles available in local languages. Arrange for oral briefings where illiteracy is a problem.

● Improve levels of worker communication and empowerment through adopting an explicit Worker Communication system which allows for safe reporting of grievances.

● Protect the safety of the worker and union representatives by providing safe reporting mechanisms and monitoring.

● Demonstrate active follow-up of reported grievances and cases of harassment or discrimination.

● Be prepared to raise concerns of employee persecution by state authorities with relevant government officials through quiet diplomacy or speaking out when the need demands.

● In countries where union activity is illegal, explore means of alternative worker representation systems within the factory or installation. Consult with international and local NGOs and labour organisations as to appropriate frameworks. Establish partnerships where useful.

● Use independent verification and monitoring to ensure continuous improvement in the area of labour standards, worker representation, and responding to grievances and cases of worker maltreatment.

● Provide training for company staff to be aware of how to tackle the challenges of child labour in a variety of situations, such as dealing with joint-venture partners, opposition from local authorities, criticism from local NGOs or pressure groups. Consider bringing in relevant NGOs and others to provide elements of the training or briefing.

Reebok – respecting freedom of association?

For the full Reebok case study, see Part II

Reebok International Ltd is a US-based leading worldwide designer, marketer and distributor of sports, fitness and casual footwear, apparel and equipment. It has taken the following steps in addressing the question of freedom of association and collective bargaining;

1. **Explicit commitment to the principles:** Reebok is unusual in that it has accepted the principles of freedom of association and collective bargaining and in selected ways is seeking to implement them (and other standards) through a model of worker empowerment.

2. **Guaranteeing worker communication:** Reebok launched its Worker Communication System (WCS) in 1997 in order to provide workers with a secure system to express workplace concerns in a manner which allowed Reebok and factory management to focus on specific issues at the time they came up. An early and critical step was to ensure factory managers would not harass workers for contacting Reebok and that a manager would not

participate in an investigation of a complaint if he/she was the subject of that complaint. Part of the challenge was to get workers to use the system and to be confident that there would no negative repercussions from using such a system.

3. **Protecting the welfare of union representatives:** Aware that freedom of association and the right to collective bargaining are only possible if union representatives are able to perform their role, Reebok has consciously chosen to seek to ensure that these workers are not harassed or discriminated against and has facilitated the development of leadership capacity amongst union activists.

4. **Public advocacy:** Reebok's willingness to push the boundaries was demonstrated in the CEO's public appeal to the President of Indonesia at the time, Habibie, to release the prominent labour rights activist, Dita Sari.

Source: Doug Cahn, Vice President for Human Rights, Reebok

Civil and Political rights of trade unionists

In its 1999 survey of violations of trade union rights the previous year, the International Confederation of Free Trade Unions (ICFTU) documents the cases of 123 workers who were murdered for their trade union activities in 1998. A further 1,650 were attacked and injured, 3,660 were arrested and 21,427 were sacked for their trade union activities. The following country-specific examples of violations of the human rights of trade unionists are indicative of the need for companies to be prepared to act for their own employees, as well as sub-contracted and joint venture staff, in cases of arrest and detention without due procedure, or in the case of unexplained disappearance:

In 1998 ...

- Latin America is the most dangerous continent for trade unionists. 98 were murdered in Colombia, seven in Bolivia and three in Ecuador. In Colombia, trade unionists from every sector were murdered, and thousands more received death threats.

- Five Indian trade unionists died after being shot by police during a peaceful demonstration outside a textile mill in Dharuhera in February.

- In Kenya, there were numerous instances of police brutality during demonstrations.

- Workers in Indonesia were beaten with rattan sticks by police to prevent them marching to the local ILO office to protest at layoffs in August.

- In Croatia workers were hospitalised after police in riot gear used water cannons to disperse a demonstration over deteriorating social conditions which took place in February.

- In Kazakhstan, 200 workers were arrested for marching to demand payment of their wages, which were three years in arrears. The government then passed a law outlawing marches and public meetings.

- In Korea, the government arrested 488 members of the KCTU union, many of whom had been protesting about job losses.

- The Chinese government has a tendency to detain any worker who seeks freedom from the straitjacket of the government-sponsored ACFTU. Hundreds of demonstrators were arrested for protesting at these detentions.

- In South Africa the police used apartheid-era laws to arrest 300 workers who had been demonstrating for better pay and conditions.

Child Labour

The international standards

The UN Convention on the Rights of the Child (CRC), the most widely ratified
human rights treaty to date, asserts that *"the Child has the right to be protected from
work that threatens his or her health, education or development. The State shall set
minimum ages for employment and regulate working conditions."* (It is noteworthy that,
to date, only two countries have not signed and ratified this convention; Somalia has
not signed or ratified, and the US has signed but not ratified.) The key principle of the
CRC is that the best interests of the child should be paramount at all times. Many
interpret this convention as implying that 'child work' (which many would
differentiate from 'child labour') *"is not necessarily exploitative and can play a positive
role in a child's development"* under certain conditions. These are: a) if the child is
above the minimum age; b) if the child is undertaking light work in regulated
conditions; c) if the work does not interfere with the child's education. A further
implication is that action to eliminate child labour should ensure that child workers'
welfare is protected and promoted at all times.

Two of the ILO core conventions define what constitutes acceptable ages and
conditions for employment. Convention No. 138 on the Minimum Age stipulates that
the minimum age for admission to employment shall not be less than the age of
completion of compulsory schooling. The convention specifies a minimum age of 15,
but there are procedures for developing nations to apply for permission to drop this to
14 and also to allow children over 12 to undertake 'light work'. All member
governments of the ILO have now ratified a new Convention, No. 182 on The Worst
Forms of Child Labour (1999) and Recommendation No. 190 on the Worst Forms of
Child Labour (1999). Directed at all people under age 18, the intention is to prohibit
and immediately eliminate:
- All forms of slavery, the sale and trafficking in children, forced or compulsory
  labour, debt bondage or serfdom.
- The use, procuring or offering a child for child prostitution or pornography.
- The use, procuring or offering a child for illegal activities, including the production
  and traffic in drugs.
- Any other work which seriously jeopardises the health, safety or morals of children,
  namely work underground, under water or at dangerous heights, work with
  dangerous machinery or tools, or the transport of heavy loads, exposure to
  hazardous substances, agents or processes, and work for long hours

The debate

With the UK and other OECD governments gearing up to put child labour at the top
of the international agenda on labour, the ILO acknowledges that child labour is a
complex problem. This complexity is reflected in the standards that define what is
legal. Debate continues between those who take an absolutist approach to abolishing
all forms of child labour and those who believe that access to work is an economic
necessity for many children and their families. The latter focus their efforts on
abolishing exploitative labour and developing improved access to education and
compensating for lost earnings.

Recommendations for companies tackling the problem of child labour:

● Take, as a starting point, the UN Convention on the Rights of the Child, ILO Convention No. 182 and ILO Recommendation No. 190, both on The Worst Forms of Child Labour.

● Consult widely with international and local NGOs and other community organisations on approaches to reducing and eventually eliminating the problem of child labour in the particular localities where the company is operating. Stakeholder consultation is an essential element of pre-investment risk assessment.

● Incorporate company principles into all contracts with joint venture partners and sub-contractors, and build these principles into monitoring of business partners' practices.

● Establish cross-sector partnerships with NGOs, private sector and government where possible to address the problems collaboratively. Local ownership of such initiatives is likely to make them more sustainable and successful. These initiatives may include flexible education provision for working children, childcare provision for working mothers, vocational training schemes for family members to boost employment opportunities for those of working age.

● Consider joining an international alliance to combat the problem constructively, thereby publicly demonstrating corporate commitment and even leadership.

● Seek company commitment at the highest level to advocate responsible business in the area of child labour. If the CEO is not willing to speak out about the company's position on this issue, NGOs and the media are likely to question the company's real commitment to tackling the problem.

● Set up systems for regular internal and independent monitoring, verification and reporting.

● Provide training for staff internally to be aware of how to tackle the challenges of child labour in a variety of situations, such as dealing with joint-venture partners, opposition from local authorities, criticism from local NGOs or pressure groups. Consider bringing in relevant NGOs and others to provide elements of the training or briefing.

The experience of **Pentland Group** in tackling the problem of child labour

For the full Pentland case study, see Part II

Pentland Group plc, a UK-based company owns a number of brands in the sportswear and clothing sectors, such as Speedo, Ellesse and Mitre. It also services a number of 'own label' footwear and clothing companies. Sourcing footballs from suppliers in Pakistan, the company has proactively tackled the problem of child labour.

1. International pressure: When the issue of child labour in Pakistan came to a head in the mid-1990s, it was the sportswear sector that attracted most international attention, as it was considered more vulnerable to consumer pressure. An international campaign was initiated by the trade union movement and supported by some US-based human rights NGOs.

2. Assessing options: For several reasons Pentland rejected the option to terminate contracts with suppliers who may have been using child labour. Walking away from the problem would not improve the situation in the factories in Pakistan. Pentland drew lessons from the case of Bangladesh in 1993-4 when, faced with a possible US boycott because of their use of child labour, Bangladeshi manufacturers laid off some 50,000 children. Thousands of those children are likely to have fallen through the inadequate social safety net, forced instead into less well paid and even more dangerous forms of work

including domestic service, breaking rocks, brick making, street vending and prostitution.

3. Constructive engagement: Pentland adopted a 'constructive engagement' approach, seeking to work with factory managers to bring standards to an acceptable level in an acceptable time period. Stages in this process have included:

• Forming an international alliance with members of the World Federation of Sporting Goods Industry, industry associations, UN bodies and NGOs, focusing on two projects; (i) workplace prevention and monitoring of child labour, (ii) social protection and rehabilitation for working children.

• Gaining local ownership for the programmes through the Sialkot Chamber of Commerce and local NGOs.

• Keeping channels of communication open with all stakeholders, including the trade unions.

• Learning from pilot projects and benchmarking progress at the factory level

• Working with suppliers to assess and manage risk through practical guidelines and training

• Demonstrating leadership within the sportswear sector to work collectively to improve standards in factories.

Source: Lesley Roberts, Group Business Standards Manager, Pentland Group

Achieving decent working conditions

> **?**
>
> **Do the working conditions in your factories or plants meet international standards? How about those of your suppliers and sub-contractors?**

The international standards

The Occupational Safety and Health Convention, 1981, (No. 155) is not one of the ILO core conventions, but it is nevertheless a major focus of the ILO's work. The stipulations laid out in this convention have been widely adopted in other model codes of conduct, such as Social Accountability 8000 (SA8000, see Section 4.3) and the Ethical Trading Initiative (ETI, see Section 4.5). Companies are called on to *provide a safe and healthy working environment*, and to *take adequate steps to prevent accidents and injury to health arising out of, associated with or occurring in the course of work, by minimising, so far as is reasonably practicable, the causes of hazards inherent in the working environment.*

Both ETI and SA8000 also require companies to *bear in mind the prevailing knowledge of the industry and of any specific hazards*; appoint a senior management representative to be responsible for the health and safety of all personnel; provide *regular and recorded health and safety training* to all personnel (and repeat this as workers are newly recruited or re-assigned); provide, for use by all personnel, clean bathrooms, access to potable water, and, if appropriate, sanitary facilities for food storage; and make sure that *accommodation, where provided, shall be clean, safe, and meet the basic needs of the workers.'*

The ILO has agreed a Convention on Minimum Wage Fixing, 1970 (No. 131) but both ETI and SA8000 have stipulated that the company should pay whichever is the higher, industry benchmark standards or the national legal minimum. In addition both stipulate that the amount should be enough to meet basic human needs and provide some discretionary income, reflecting the on-going debate about a 'living wage'.

Recommendations for companies seeking to meet international standards of working conditions

A company's influence over working conditions obviously lessens as it moves away from its direct operations to joint venture partners and sub-contractors down the supply chain. Nevertheless, society at large will hold a company responsible for violations occurring in plants from which it sources products or services, and therefore over which it has a degree of influence. Those companies which claim to be responsible or 'ethical' in their sourcing practices will be held up to particular scrutiny. The following considerations should be taken into account in addressing working conditions:

● Labour rights under the umbrella of 'working conditions' range from health and safety to fair wage provision. When drawing up company principles and guidelines, take into account ILO Convention No. 155 on Occupational Health and Safety, No. 131 on Minimum Wage Fixing, and be aware of the debate among unions, NGOs and governments on what constitutes the 'living wage'. Other ILO conventions cover issues such as discrimination, treatment of women, right to leisure time. They provide a good basis on which to build company human rights policy.

● Incorporate company principles into all contracts with joint venture partners and sub-contractors, and build these principles into monitoring of business partners' practices.

● Ensure workers are aware of their rights through making company principles available in local languages. Arrange for oral briefings where illiteracy is a problem.

● Improve levels of worker communication and empowerment through adopting an explicit Worker Communication system which allows for safe reporting of grievances.

● Consult with international and local NGOs and labour organisations to explore possibilities of partnership initiatives to finding solutions to problems, such as micro-credit schemes for financially insecure homeworkers far down the supply chain.

● Consider working collaboratively with other companies and relevant government ministries in the sector to raise standards of health and safety for example.

● Consult regularly from the outset with local management as to how to achieve continuous improvement and, therefore, competitiveness. Encourage a sense of local ownership by the factory or site manager.

● External verification, monitoring and reporting is essential not only within a company's core operations, but also down the supply chain. Relevant NGOs can provide very useful skills and independence in this work.

● Training on working conditions which brings together buyers and suppliers underpins a company's commitment to attaining high standards in this field. Joint training builds trust, broadens understanding of each other's needs and requirements, and establishes a framework for collaborative improvement.

B&Q – addressing working conditions

For the full B&Q case study, see Part II

B&Q is a UK-based DIY manufacturer and retailer with a turnover of £1.96 billion in 1998. It has building, decorative, electrical and hardware product lines, many of which are made in the informal sector or in cottage industry units.

1. Health and Safety: The initial drive to address Health and Safety (H&S) conditions came in the early 1990s from within B&Q, with its managers taking a strategic decision to extend the scope of its environmental audit to cover H&S conditions. The Chairman and Board took an active leadership role in this process. B&Q managers acknowledge that health and safety is a non-controversial point of departure for companies addressing working conditions more broadly.

2. Taking responsibility: Based on its experience in tackling environmental problems, B&Q rejected the boycott option and chose instead to consolidate contracts with a supplier whom it considered most likely to take the required action. It was considered important that the H&S and environmental teams worked independently of the company's buyers to ensure impartiality.

3. Forming local partnerships: In India B&Q's Environment team chose an appropriate Indian NGO partner through the networks of a UK-based international fair trade organisation. The NGO partner brought local expertise and experience in promoting fair trade for cottage industry producers.

4. Developing audit tools: B&Q expanded their Supplier Environmental Audit whereby suppliers are graded to incorporate working conditions. According to the results, B&Q has a framework for response to the supplier, ranging from termination of the contract through to close partnership with local management to improve standards.

Source: Dr. Alan Knight,
Environmental Coordinator, B&Q

Bonded and forced labour

Are you operating in a country where forced or bonded labour is a problem? Is there any way that your company is connected, directly or indirectly, with forced or bonded labour?

The international standards

Bonded labour, also known as debt bondage, is one of the oldest forms of slavery and, despite being illegal almost everywhere, still affects millions of adults and children and migrant workers. The UDHR states "no-one shall be held in slavery or servitude; slavery and the slave trade shall be prohibited in all their forms". Bonded labour is outlawed by the United Nations under Article 1(b) of the 1956 Supplementary Convention on the Abolition of Slavery, the Slave Trade and Institutions and Practices Similar to Slavery. It is also taken by the ILO as one of the practices to be eradicated under Convention No. 29 on Forced Labour.

The problem

Forms of bonded labour are found all over the world, but it is most common in the South Asian countries of India, Pakistan and Nepal where it has its roots in the caste system and feudal agricultural relationships. It is common in agriculture in these countries, both on small farms and on large estates producing for export, and in brick making and stone quarrying. Around the world it is also used as a method of controlling and retaining cheap labour, often linked to migration.

There is no simple guide to identifying the use of bonded labour, but companies need to be aware of the possibilities when monitoring suppliers for acceptable labour standards. The examples below may offer some insight into the problem:

- USA fashion companies have been purchasing finished items of clothing from operations based in Saipan, an offshore American "commonwealth" in the Pacific Mariana Islands. Workers in the factories are migrants from Bangladesh, China, Philippines and Thailand. They have often taken a loan to pay the fee to an agency for finding the job. The loan is used as a way of forcing the employees to work very long hours or offset against their agreed pay in ways solely under the control of the employer. Some US importers are currently being sued by the employees for various illegal employment practices under US law.

- During the 1980s the hand-knotted carpet industry in South Asia boomed with demand from Europe and the USA. Many thousands of looms were set up in the Indian State of Uttar Pradesh. Cheap child labour was imported from the neighbouring State of Bihar to operate the looms, and many of the children were bonded in exchange for small advances given to their parents. Importing companies purchased through Indian exporters who used middlemen to arrange for the carpets to be made in remote weaving sheds containing only a few looms. Importers were then surprised to find themselves pilloried for selling carpets made by bonded child labour. Similar forms of bonded labour may be found in other exports from the region where materials are produced by small businesses working as sub-contractors. Exports of agricultural products from estates in the region, such as sugar, may also have been produced by bonded labour.

In the case of forced labour, whereby the workers are obliged by the state to carry out a certain kind of work, companies can be incriminated by association. Any company operating in Myanmar (Burma) may find itself benefiting indirectly from forced labour and portering that has been used by state authorities on infrastructure projects. In 1999 member governments of the International Labour Organisation adopted a resolution citing Myanmar for consistent violations of the Forced Labour Convention. The resolution imposed sanctions in the form of the withholding of technical cooperation and other forms of assistance from the ILO.

Companies may not be aware that certain components of products they source from a particular country, such as China, have been produced by captive or prison labour. Credible monitoring of working conditions in detention is usually impossible, but some human rights NGOs have been able to document abusive forms of captive labour in some countries. Companies should make every effort to ensure that any goods they source from these countries are not produced by prison labour. This can be partially achieved by rigorous monitoring of the supply chain and consultation with NGOs and worker representatives. Companies should also consult Amnesty International and Human Rights Watch reports on this issue.

Recommendations

- ILO Convention 29 on Forced Labour provides an important starting point for companies operating in countries where bonded labour is known to be a problem.

- Companies must develop checking procedures that involve good consultation and co-operation with local trade unions and NGOs working in the neighbourhood of their suppliers. Only in this way can companies obtain a detailed understanding of employment practices covering the localities, factories and suppliers in question. Indications that wages and/or working hours are linked to the repayment of loans or advances on wages should be seen as a danger signal, requiring detailed investigation. Consultation is an essential element of the pre-investment risk assessment and on-going monitoring of the situation.

- Companies should be aware that bonded labour can also be involved when suppliers claim that all workers are self-employed. Consultation with community organisations and NGOs is essential in investigating this risk.

- Transnational companies (TNCs) operating in countries where bonded or forced labour is known to be a problem should undertake extensive stakeholder consultation and independent monitoring of the company's operations. Where possible this should be undertaken with joint venture partners and sub-contractors as well.

- Country managers should also be prepared to raise concerns regarding bonded or forced labour directly with the host government at an appropriate level. Acting collectively with other TNCs to raise concerns with the government lessens the risk of exposure to the individual company.

- Training for buyers and suppliers on this issue is important to raise awareness of the risks to the company, the opportunities for tackling and finding solutions to the problem. Relevant NGOs have a useful role to play in this training process.

Source: David Ould, Anti-Slavery International, London, UK

3. Principles to practice

3. Principles to practice

How are companies moving beyond the rhetoric to embed human rights in a company's operations at all levels? This section explores the experiences of several companies in developing and implementing a human rights policy. The key elements to be drawn out from these reinforce recommendations made in previous sections and may be summarised as follows:

Key elements in putting human rights principles into practice

- An explicit commitment to support principles enshrined in the Universal Declaration of Human Rights is an important starting point.

- Companies should recognise that human rights do not occur in a vacuum. They are part of a continuum of responsible practices that encompass employees, communities and other stakeholders. In this respect, it is important that the links between complementary or potentially conflicting internal company policies be addressed.

- Assigning responsibility for the development and implementation of the human rights policy to a central function within the company should ensure appropriate integration of human rights considerations into the overall business decision-making process.

- In developing policies and practices with regard to human rights, it is important that companies clearly delineate the boundaries of their responsibilities or willingness to become involved in advocacy or exert influence. This clarifies the extent of assumed responsibilities and makes it possible to monitor progress against objectives and targets.

- Assurance processes should be implemented to ensure that the human rights policy is being adhered to and that companies' operations are being evaluated for their potential impacts on human rights.

- If companies are serious about monitoring their human rights performance, it is critically important that they develop mechanisms for systematically reporting on progress. Independent monitoring and verification by a credible social auditor is important for external legitimacy.

- Cross-sector partnerships offer potentially powerful mechanisms for developing and implementing human rights strategies. The potential for such partnerships with NGOs or community groups should be explored at various levels, from investment decision-making through to local monitoring of human rights conditions or peace-building initiatives.

- Engaging in constructive dialogue with critics can be very important. Companies which have reacted defensively to criticism in the media and from NGOs, and which have denied allegations of human rights violations without offering to enter into discussion, have often been the target of even more vigorous criticism. Whether founded or not, such criticism can be damaging to corporate reputation.

A number of leading TNCs are addressing the challenges of translating their commitments to uphold human rights principles into operational practice. Some are further along this road than others. The following summaries highlight some key steps companies have taken in this process, and important lessons learned.

BP Amoco – Exerting positive influence?

For the full case study, see Part II

1. Recognising international human rights standards

BP Amoco's Ethical Conduct Policy explicitly supports the principles set forth in the UN Universal Declaration on Human Rights and the ILO Tripartite Declaration of Principles concerning Multinational Enterprises and Social Policy. In addition its Relationships Policy commits the company to demonstrating respect for human dignity and the rights of individuals.

2. Conducting country risk reviews

BP Amoco now conducts a Country Risk Review. Amongst other factors, this process takes into consideration the social, political, cultural and human rights context of the country using a 20-year planning horizon. Market and shareholder risks are also important factors in the process, as are potential reputational risks. The process involves a select number of internal staff from business units and the corporate centre, as well as external experts.

3. The Rule of Law

BP Amoco respects the rule of law, recognising the hierarchy of international, regional, national and local laws. The company supports the establishment of the rule of law. Sound laws create greater investment certainty and reduce risk.

4. Resolving conflicts

The Relationship Policy guidelines are more explicit in committing the company, as part of its relations with governments, to work in partnership with others to resolve tensions or conflicts arising between international expectations on human rights and local or national practice. BP Amoco views this commitment as part of its mandate to make a constructive contribution to society.

5. Ultimate step of disinvestment

Where human rights abuses are of concern, BP Amoco's preference is to stay and engage rather than disinvest. *"The two main exceptions"* says David Rice, Director of BP Amoco's Government and Public Affairs Policy Unit, *"are where our ability to maintain the safety and security of employees is compromised, and where it becomes impossible to operate in accordance with business policies".*

Source: David Rice, Director Government and Public Affairs Policy Unit, BP Amoco

---

Rio Tinto – Facing the challenge of implementation

For the full case study, see Part II.

1. Policy commitment to human rights

Rio Tinto first published its human rights policy in early 1998 in the company's statement of Business Practice, *'The way we work'*. The motivation for explicitly articulating the values of the company was in part to help establish Rio Tinto as the 'developer of choice' — in line with its stated objective — and in part to respond to society's increasing expectations of natural resource developers as corporate citizens.

2. Internal primer

Specifically in the human rights arena, an internal primer is being prepared to demonstrate the relevance of human rights to the operations. The primer will also illustrate practical approaches to dealing with human rights issues for operational staff.

3. Review of assurance mechanisms

An internal review of assurance mechanisms is also in progress that is starting to identify areas for improvement and possible approaches. Options under consideration include external verification of community engagement and a system of internal assurance letters devoted to the company's social policies.

4. Opposing infringements of human rights

As well as referring to the company's support for the Universal Declaration, Rio Tinto's Human Rights Policy specifically requires the operations to oppose infringements of the rights of employees and local communities. Operations encountering such cases are required to draw up a strategy for dealing with them, either through private dialogue, public action, or a combination of both.

Source: Robert Court, Head of Government Relations, Rio Tinto

The case of **Levi Strauss & Co.** – forming multi-stakeholder partnerships

For the full case study, see Part II

Levi Strauss & Co. (a privately-owned US company) is the world's largest brand-name apparel manufacturer with sales in 1998 of $6 billion. The company owns brands including Levi's, Dockers and Slates and employs 30,000 people world-wide. It has a head start on many human and labour rights issues given that it was the first transnational to adopt a code. It has also consistently used a multi-stakeholder approach to develop and implement its policy on working conditions.

1. An evolving process of monitoring: In recent years, Levi Strauss has experimented with intensive forms of multi-stakeholder engagement. This is part of the evolution of an internal monitoring process that has gone from a simple Q&A session to a detailed review about implementing the key human rights elements of its policy. The most recent step has been a pilot project in the Dominican Republic (DR) which was designed to help answer the question of how to make internal monitoring more effective and therefore credible.

2. The cross-sector partnership approach: Professional auditors can be expensive, may fail to understand the local situation well enough, can have insufficient access to workers to be able to verify the most important human rights issues, and can have limited credibility for the social verification task. Unions are perhaps the obvious 'social partner' for this sort of work but the business-union relationship is often very tense, with an adversarial history. Labour-friendly NGOs who have the credibility to verify working conditions, are often not well equipped for the task. And those NGOs who have the best capacity and credibility for this role often have the least developed relationship with contractors. Bringing all parties together around the table seemed to be the most constructive way forward for monitoring.

3. Building contractor support and ownership: The Levi Strauss in-country managers met with their DR contractors to determine whether an innovative partnership could be developed between the company, its contractors and NGOs. All four contractors signed up to the project.

4. Choosing appropriate NGO partners: It was crucial to the success of the process that NGOs did not feel they were being used for PR purposes or for sub-contracted services, but that they could maintain their independence within the partnership. The NGOs selected represented a range of focus areas from development programmes to women's issues, and all had proven local credibility. Notwithstanding the challenge of working with different organisations and their varying cultures, the process has succeeded in building confidence in the auditing and identifying key areas for improvement, such as more worker involvement in the monitoring of the contractors' codes of conduct. Long-term relationships have been established between the contractors and the NGOs, indicating the sustainability of this partnership approach.

5. Improved performance for the contractors: one of Levi Strauss' contractors in the Dominican Republic, Grupo M, acknowledged that their motivation at the start was *"to do what the customer wanted. Over time we began to see very real benefits – workers respond so well to this kind of approach. So we have now gone well beyond Levi Strauss' requirements"*. These benefits have improved the contractor's bottom line – significantly reduced absenteeism, no strikes, ability to win contracts from other major brands. The contractors acknowledge that top management commitment was the key to getting the whole project off the ground.

Source: Miriam Rodriguez, Latin America Regional Manager, Levi Strauss & Co.

4. Drivers of change

4. Drivers of change

The pressures that companies are facing to demonstrate a commitment to human rights have been building up across several fronts. This section analyses each of the main pressure points, using practical examples to illustrate how they have contributed to raising the profile of human rights on the corporate agenda.

4.1 Shareholder pressure

Shareholder resolutions and annual general meetings

Shareholder resolutions about social issues rarely succeed in terms of being approved by a majority of shareholders, but they do draw attention to such issues and add to the pressure on companies. Shareholder concerns about human rights issues have also led to shareholder resolutions at corporate annual meetings and demonstrations outside those meetings, frustrating company managers by putting them on the defensive in a forum that they intended to be an orchestrated showcase of their company's achievements.

Cited below are just two examples of corporate action resulting from shareholder concerns:

- At the company's May 14 1998 annual meeting, Mobil Chairman Lucio Noto stated that he would bring up with the Nigerian military junta the cases of two imprisoned oil workers union leaders: Milton Dabibi and Frank Kokori. This statement came in response to a question directed to Mr. Noto by Cordelia Kokori, Frank Kokori's daughter. Both union leaders have since been freed as Nigeria's new military rulers have released nearly all political prisoners.
- On August 11 1998, ARCO announced that it would completely withdraw from Myanmar. The company maintained that it was pulling out for business reasons only. However, it is highly likely that the escalating campaign had some impact on ARCO's decision.

Changing legislation is beginning to reflect those ethical concerns expressed by shareholders. In 1998 the US Securities & Exchange Commission (SEC) decided that companies should not be allowed to exclude shareholder resolutions raising workplace issues and matters of significant social policy. This decision was a victory for social and environmental organisations and concerned shareholders, who had joined in an intense lobbying campaign aimed at getting the SEC to reverse its restrictive 1992 ruling.

The Interfaith Center on Corporate Responsibility (ICCR) regularly publishes information about shareholder resolutions related to social responsibility. A recent ICCR publication profiled 224 shareholder resolutions to 151 companies in 1999.[1] A number of these resolutions related to human rights issues, for example the following resolutions concern human rights in China:

i) **Boeing:** The resolution asks Boeing to adopt *"basic human rights criteria for its business operation in and/or with the People's Republic of China"* and to describe how it intends to implement them.

ii) **Exxon:** The resolution asks Exxon, in relation to an exploration venture in China, to review its *"code of business conduct with the view to including in it an explicit commitment to human rights, social justice and environmental responsibility"* towards the communities in which the company operates.

iii) **General Motors and Lucent Technology:** Resolutions ask each company to adopt *"policies for all dealings with China,"* including that it will not accept goods or services produced by slave or forced labour, not sell to any facility using slave or

1. Interfaith Center on Corporate Responsibility, "Corporate Social Responsibility Challenges 1999," *The Corporate Examiner*, Vol. 28, No. 3-4 (Mar. 1999).

forced labour, and will pursue the right to on-site inspections to determine the existence of slave or forced labour.

iv) Morgan Stanley: The resolution refers to Morgan Stanley having underwritten bonds for China's State Development Bank, which loaned funds for the controversial Three Gorges dam. The resolution asks Morgan Stanley to report on its underwriting, investing and lending criteria, *"with the view to incorporating criteria related to a transaction's impact on the environment, human rights and risk to the company's reputation."*

Source: Christopher Avery, Business and Human Rights in a Time of Change, February 2000, Amnesty International UK

Ethical and socially responsible investment

Socially responsible investment is nothing new – parts of the religious and NGO communities have been practising it for decades. What is new, however, is the importance that mainstream business and financial institutions are now attaching to it. It is beginning to impinge on corporate consciousness in ways that were unthinkable a few years ago.

Investments in ethically screened portfolios have nearly doubled in the US over the past two years to $2.1 trillion, according to the 1999 report of the Social Investment Forum. This is twice the level of growth of total US funds under management during the same period.

The report also reveals that 13% of professionally managed investments in the US now use socially responsible investment criteria, compared with 9% in 1997.

In the UK, there has also been a rapid growth in the number of funds investing according to ethical criteria. This is likely to take a further leap forward in response to a new regulatory requirement. From July 2000 all UK pension funds are obliged to indicate in their annual reports the extent to which social, environmental and ethical considerations are taken into account in investment decisions, if at all. Pension funds that have no ethical framework may find themselves under pressure from their members to develop such a policy in conjunction with their fund managers.

The President of Calvert Group, which operates socially responsible funds in the US, predicted in 1994 the increasing importance of human rights in socially responsible investment decisions:

> *SRI (socially responsible investing) funds with stringent criteria in the area of human rights actively seek out companies that are making serious efforts to promote human rights at home and abroad. This may take the form of developing policies and programmes that follow higher standards than those required in host countries or adopting explicit human rights principles to guide their international operations…*
> *As the world moves ever closer to becoming a truly integrated global economy, human rights and the other key aspects of the behaviour of companies are likely to take on increased importance for more and more investors who will demand just as much emphasis on people as on profits.*

Organisations that provide social screening information to funds and investors are increasingly including human rights as one of the factors in their assessment of a company's record.

Source: Christopher Avery, Business and Human Rights in a Time of Change, February 2000, Amnesty International UK

The profiles which follow indicate how and why a number of investment research bodies and major asset managers are starting to incorporate human rights into investment criteria.

Ethical Investment Research Information Service (EIRIS): responding to investor demand on human rights

EIRIS is a UK-based not-for-profit research organisation, established in 1983 with assistance from a number of churches. It now caters to a broad spectrum of clients including unit trusts, pension funds and charities. Human rights are not only an important consideration for many ethical investors, but are beginning to impinge on the consciousness of the general public. An NOP survey which EIRIS commissioned in June 1999, revealed that 56% of respondents would object to their pension funds investing in companies operating in countries with oppressive governments. 47% of respondents would look more favourably on companies conducting business in those countries provided that they were developing policies which reflected the human rights context of their operations.

In the past, EIRIS would assess companies on the basis of their presence in countries where human rights violations were widespread. More recently, EIRIS has been developing new company-specific human rights criteria that consider what companies are actually doing to integrate human rights into their policies and practices. This is a fundamental shift, taking into account changing perceptions on the part of ethical investors. They are becoming less concerned about where a company operates, and more concerned about the positive steps that are being taken to prevent complicity in violations and to further human rights actively. There are five aspects of a company's impact of particular concern to EIRIS:
- employment conditions
- product sourcing
- civil and political rights
- policies governing the use of armed security personnel
- management systems and auditing procedures

Companies will only be asked to provide information on categories relevant to their type of business. A grading system, reflecting the steps companies are taking to address human rights concerns, will be made available to investors. It is anticipated that EIRIS's clients will look favourably on those companies that have made in-roads to address issues that lie within their sphere of influence.

EIRIS recognises that human rights are a new consideration for businesses and that relatively few have even begun to look at these concerns. This has been taken into account in devising the new terms of reference. EIRIS's human rights criteria for the year 2000 are only the start of the process. It is envisaged that within a few years, the level of sophistication of human rights policies, management information systems and reporting practices will match what is now available on environmental matters. As standards rise, so too will the expectations of the ethical investment community. As ethical investment mushrooms, EIRIS expects that a growing number of companies will respond to consumer demand and integrate social considerations into their standard business calculations. The inextricable links between a company's share value and its reputation is likely to ensure that in future it will not be financially viable to neglect human rights concerns.

Source: Lucy Amis, researcher, Ethical Investment Research Information Service, London, UK

The role of the **Pensions Investment Research Consultants** (PIRC) in advising institutional investors

PIRC is the UK's leading investment adviser to institutional investors on corporate governance and corporate responsibility issues, with clients holding assets in excess of £200 billion. PIRC's approach to human rights centres on the premise that shareholders can play a constructive and vital role in influencing company behaviour, policy and practice. As such, they use formal instruments of ownership and control, such as the exercise of voting rights, and more informal methods of engagement, such as dialogue and negotiation in order to improve corporate policy.

PIRC has launched a Corporate Responsibility Service for institutional investors which includes policy advice, benchmarking, company and sector profiles, issues briefings and organises conferences on a range of stakeholder issues including such human rights concerns as child labour, repressive governments and arms.

In its role as the secretariat for the Local Authority Pension Fund Forum (LAPFF), PIRC has also played a leading role in many of the high-profile shareholder campaigns of the last decade, including those surrounding apartheid in South Africa, the *maquiladoras*, Shell in Nigeria, and overseas labour standards.

In May 1997, LAPFF and PIRC in conjunction with the ECCR, in response to Shell's activities in the Ogoni region of Nigeria, took the rare and innovative step of putting forward a corporate responsibility shareholder resolution to the AGM. The resolution called for Shell to establish an independent external audit of its human rights and environmental policies and to report on these issues across the Shell group of companies. The motion succeeded in garnering an impressive level of support, with 17% of the votes cast, some 64.8 million shares voted, withholding support from the board. Although defeated, the resolution had the effect of helping to persuade Shell to adopt best practice on environmental and human rights policies with management systems and reporting mechanisms in place to provide shareholders with a robust framework for monitoring and tracking progress.

In its most recent campaign, LAPFF and PIRC have written to over fifty UK listed retail firms requesting information about their policies on child labour and overseas employment standards throughout the supply chain. The campaign is designed to encourage such groups to adopt codes of conduct and policies which encompass the core ILO conventions. The campaign will, on the basis of responses, publicise those companies which are either moving towards best practice or taking positive steps. For companies which refuse to engage or cooperate in the campaign, LAPFF and PIRC will work hard to ensure that they do take these legitimate issues seriously and develop appropriate policies, with shareholder action remaining a potentially forceful course of remedial action.

Source: Stuart Bell, Research Director, Pensions Investment Research Consultants, London, UK

Human rights engagement – view from **Friends Provident**

Friends Provident has been managing socially responsible investment funds for 15 years, making it Europe's oldest and biggest provider of such funds. Today, through its asset management subsidiary, Friends, Ivory and Sime, Friends Provident manages £2 billion in its ethical funds.

Traditionally socially responsible investment has tended to avoid investing in companies facing human rights challenges (as well as a range of other 'ethical' issues). Friends Provident is now trying to develop a more constructive approach by 'engaging' with companies in which it invests that are facing such challenges, and to work with them to encourage good practice.

Friends Provident believes that addressing and managing human rights issues is increasingly becoming an essential element of good business practice, especially for multinational companies. These companies can face a number of significant business risks when they operate in countries with poor human rights records – which have the potential to damage the company's financial performance.

For companies in which Friends Provident invests, the goals of the human rights engagement programme are to:
● work with those companies to identify ways in which they might protect or enhance their reputation and shareholder value through good management of human rights issues
● encourage those companies to publish and uphold strong human rights policies

More generally, Friends Provident is keen to contribute to the debate around human rights and corporate responsibility by raising the issue's profile in the business community. To this end, Friends Provident is collaborating with several leading organisations in developing the engagement programme, including the Prince of Wales Business Leaders Forum, New Economics Foundation, Ashridge Centre for Business and Society and Amnesty International UK.

Source: Rachel Crossley, Ethics Policy Analyst, Friends Provident, London, UK

Incorporating human rights criteria into investment decisions – view from **Storebrand**

The Storebrand Scudder Environmental Value Fund (EVF) managed by the Norwegian company, Storebrand, is a diversified equity portfolio of companies around the world and across industries that set the highest standards of environmental responsibility. In 1997, the EVF incorporated social and ethical dimensions into its Sustainability Index. Working on the basis that corporations have an obligation, albeit not legally binding, to uphold and promote human rights in every country in which they operate, EVF has developed a generic set of criteria that can be used to evaluate the human rights performance of firms. From these criteria (listed below), the Fund will form indicators on human rights performance:

1. Human rights policy
2. Organisation of human rights activities within the corporation
3. Human rights impact assessments
4. Internal human rights practices
5. Human rights standards governing suppliers, contractors, sub-contractors and other business partners
6. Human rights standards governing a country's law enforcement institutions
7. Internal management system that encompasses human rights measures
8. Internal and independent third party auditing of human rights performance
9. Reporting on human rights activities
10. External evaluation of a corporation's human rights performance

The Fund's new qualification rule will be that a firm's environmental and human rights performance must be among the top 30% within its respective sector. Storebrand predicts that environmental, human rights and social and ethical factors will play an increasingly important role in the financial performance of a company vis-à-vis financial and strategic factors.

The EVF will be collecting evidence on the financial impacts of the incorporation of human rights criteria before implementing the above framework.

Source: Sarita Bartlett, Portfolio Manager, Storebrand, Norway

4.2 Transparency and disclosure

Greater transparency is an inescapable consequence of satellite communications technology and the global reach of the media. Increased disclosure is one of the outcomes of the debate on corporate governance, self-policing and regulation.

Human rights and development organisations are taking advantage of the communications revolution. They are using the Internet to gather and publicise information about the social record of companies worldwide. Pierre Sané, Secretary General of Amnesty International, noted recently: *"The fact is that human rights groups are now so numerous that it makes it much more difficult to suppress information, especially in the age of the Internet."*

The Economist talks of a democratisation of information via the Internet which is giving the individual citizen the real possibility of challenging business and government on environmental and social issues:

> *An old lop-sidedness in democracy – big business and big government are better informed than individuals, so win most of the big arguments – is suddenly corrected. It used to be that executives and bureaucrats could assure small-fry citizens that problems had been analysed, scientists consulted, safeguards put into place. Now citizens no longer need to accept those assurances helplessly. They can log on to the Internet and check them, with a few clicks of a mouse.* (3 April 1999)

Repressive governments continue to attempt to deny citizens their right to freedom of information by partial censorship of the Internet. In an article in The Guardian on 27 January 2000, state authorities in China, Myanmar (Burma), Jordan, Malaysia and

Sri Lanka are all cited as contributing to *"the slow spread of cyber suppression"*. Andrew Puddephatt, director of Article 19, a UK-based NGO which campaigns for freedom of expression, condemned the Chinese government's major clampdown on Internet use: *"Any attempt by any government to impose censorship of the kind commonly applied to newspapers and television networks around the world must be regarded as a very dangerous precedent."* (Guardian, 27 January 2000)

TNCs should consider issues such as the right to freedom of expression and information as part of their human rights impact assessment and monitoring, as state restrictions to these freedoms may have an impact on company employees.

Power of the Internet – view from **Control Risks Group**

The number of people using the Internet worldwide is expected to rise from some 143m in 1998 to more than 700m in 2001. The social and geographical spread of users remains uneven: the typical user is still an English-speaking middle-class male, but the medium is spreading – even in developing countries. In early 1999, the number of Internet accounts in the People's Republic of China was only 2m; by the following July the figure had doubled to 4m; and it is expected to reach 10m by the end of the year 2000.

Knowledge is power. By making all kinds of information more widely available, the Internet changes the balance of power between companies, governments, NGOs and – ultimately – ordinary people. The emergence of the new technology does not prove or disprove any particular point of view in the human rights debate, but it does lead to demands for greater accountability from organisations exercising political or economic power. Advocacy groups have been quick to seize on the benefits of the Internet. By contrast, companies are only just beginning to rise to the challenge.

A source of information

The Internet assists the human rights debate by serving as a source of information on regions which might previously have been considered obscure. Myanmar (Burma) is an example. The BurmaNet newsgroup distributes daily news bulletins culled from the regional and international press (see www.burma.net.news). The role of international oil and gas companies in Myanmar remains controversial in the human rights community, and information on the latest developments is easy to find.

Advocacy groups have made their own information readily available on the Web. For example, the websites of both Amnesty (www.amnesty.org) and Human Rights Watch (www.hrw.org) include the full set of country reports from each organisation. These are complemented by NGOs specialising in particular regions such as Human Rights in China (www.hrinchina.org) and the Tibet Information Network (www.tibetinfo.net). Other groups focus on particular issues. These include Corporate Watch (www.corpwatch.org) which monitors the activities of multinationals; or the International Rivers Network (www.irn.org), which concentrates on water issues – particularly the social and environmental repercussions of major hydroelectric projects.

A campaign tool

Advocacy groups' websites typically include 'links' both to the websites of like-minded organisations and, often enough, their opponents. These links also make it possible to co-ordinate campaigns much more effectively. In the 1970s and 1980s anti-apartheid activists co-ordinated protests through 'telephone trees', where one supporter would undertake to pass on news to, say, five others. The Internet fulfils the same function much more effectively.

In early 1998 the Council of Canadians used the Internet to publish a statement criticising the Multilateral Agreement on Investment (MAI), and this was signed by 560 NGOs in 67 countries. In the spring of 1998 the OECD suspended negotiations on the MAI, and formally dropped them the following October. From the OECD's point of view the NGO campaign had been completely unexpected, and was a significant factor in the closure of the MAI negotiations.

Companies' response

By the late 1990s many leading companies, especially those that had been particularly stung by human rights criticisms, had begun to adopt a more proactive approach.

Company websites now typically include codes of conduct or business principles, and a few have incorporated specific references to human rights. Some companies are using the Internet as a means of canvassing public views, an approach which they hope will give them advance warning of major controversies.

The Web undoubtedly serves to highlight the dilemmas associated with human rights and business. By distributing news, opinion and information on commercial best practice, it may help provide some of the answers. But this will be a long-term process, demanding effort and creativity from all sides of the Internet debate.

Source: John Bray, Principal Research Consultant, Control Risks Group, London, UK

Consumer pressure

Consumer awareness has been steadily increasing over the last five years. High-street protests, university campus boycotts, Internet campaigns, NGO action – all have contributed to pressurising companies to become more accountable on matters of human rights.

During the 1990s, grassroots consumer campaigns in the US targeted companies doing business in Myanmar, and have been regarded as important factors in some of those companies withdrawing from that country. PepsiCo announced its complete withdrawal from Myanmar after Harvard University turned down Pepsi for a $1 million contract and Stanford University decided not to allow Taco Bell (a PepsiCo restaurant) on campus after 2000 students petitioned the university to sever ties with all companies doing business in Myanmar.

The Internet has revolutionised the reach of consumer campaigns, linking pressure groups and concerned individuals worldwide in pointing their spotlight on global corporations which they consider to have fallen below international standards of good practice. Listed below are examples of just two of the many Internet-based consumer pressure groups which monitor and publicise corporate behaviour.

Role of **Corporate Watch**

Corporate Watch is a San Francisco-based online magazine designed to provide information on the social, political, economic and environmental impacts of transnational corporations.
It is a project of TRAC –
The Transnational Resource and Action Center.

In 1997, TRAC obtained a leaked internal Nike document detailing the results of Ernst & Young's labour and environmental audit of a Nike facility in Vietnam and decided to make the results public. The deteriorating conditions in the Vietnam Nike factory led to fierce media attention and damaging editorials, increasing the pressure on Nike to improve conditions in its overseas factories. Corporate Watch's campaign against Nike gave momentum to the movement to hold companies accountable for their actions.

Corporate Watch is funded partly by donations and also receives sponsorship from various foundations. Its advisory board is made up of NGOs from Central and South America, Asia and the United States.

The US-based Corporate Watch should not be confused with the Oxford-based research and publishing group of the same name. The UK group was set up in 1996 to advocate activism against multinational corporations. Corporate Watch UK produces a number of sector-specific publications as well as a quarterly magazine covering corporate activity in the UK. The magazine seeks to expose corporate crimes, inform its subscribers about current campaigns and also provide feature articles on topical issues.

Sources: Corporate Watch US, San Francisco, US
Corporate Watch UK, Oxford, UK

Role of **Sweatshop Watch**

Sweatshop Watch is a coalition of organisations concerned with labour, community and civil rights as well as religious and women's issues. The coalition is committed to eliminating the exploitation that occurs in sweatshops. It was formed in 1995 when a number of organisations came together in response to the discovery of inhumane conditions in sweatshops employing Thai immigrant workers in El Monte, California. Through several campaigns to build public support and put pressure on retailers, Sweatshop Watch was successful in winning $4 million from retailers and manufacturers for overtime compensation and damages for civil rights violations.

The coalition educates garment workers about their rights by holding regular workshops. It also uses a variety of tools, such as newsletters and a website, to educate consumers. Current work with the University Coalition Against Sweatshops is intended to ensure implementation of the University of California's *Code of Conduct for Trademark Licensees* which is designed to eliminate procurement of equipment, materials and supplies produced by forced labour, convict labour or indentured labour.

Source: www.sweatshopwatch.org

4.3 Social reporting and social auditing

A sound corporate human rights policy should involve both internal monitoring and external auditing and reporting for a number of reasons:

- to measure performance against stated objectives;
- to define areas for improvement in company operations;
- to promote transparency and accountability;
- to build trust with employees, communities and other stakeholders.

What is a social audit?

Social reporting is a relatively new way of assessing a company's impact on society. So far, only a few companies have attempted the process.

Conceptually, it differs from most traditional methods of measurement. Potentially, it covers everything from environmental emissions to personnel policies; it includes stakeholder's perceptions, and is not simply based on benchmarks chosen by the company. Social auditing presents a challenge to companies to publish fuller data than it might normally choose. In return, it can deliver a powerful reassurance about the company's ethics to its stakeholders.

Within the current corporate climate, there is growing acceptance of the notion of the triple bottom line – recognising that an organisation's performance needs to be judged in terms of its economic, environmental and social impact. Not only are leading companies beginning to measure their performance in each of these three dimensions, they are increasingly willing to report on their activities. There is a long-standing legal obligation upon businesses to report on their financial performance. In recent years, the practice of environmental reporting has also become relatively well established. However, it is only very recently that the practice of social auditing and reporting has been taken up by a few mainstream corporations.

Ashridge Centre for Business and Society (part of Ashridge Management College), based in the UK, defines a process of social audit as:

> "a mechanism by which a company's stakeholders (its employees, customers, shareholders and others) are able to judge the social performance of an organisation in relation to its stated values".

Ashridge's definition gives rise to two important issues:

- A social audit involves stakeholders – it is a process of dialogue and consultation with those groups that are considered vital to the long-term sustainable development of the organisation.

- An essential part of this dialogue should be about the nature and the meaning of the organisation's values, so that these reflect the concerns of all those affected by the company's operations.

What makes a social audit different?

Growing interest in non-financial measures of corporate success has been fuelled by management approaches such as the *'balanced scorecard'* and the *'business excellence model'* of the European Foundation for Quality Management (EFQM). As such, it is not surprising that many large companies are already carrying out a wide range of activities in order to collect information about the social impact of their business. Whether driven by statutory requirements or a desire to achieve a better understanding of the 'nature of the business', most large companies already have systems in place that could provide some of the information that would typically appear in a social audit.

However, there are a number of features that distinguish a process of social audit from existing mechanisms of accounting and reporting.

- The degree to which different stakeholders get **access to the information** that is collected and analysed, e.g. is the data purely an aid to internal decision-making or is it published and distributed to employees, shareholders, customers, suppliers, the local community?

- The degree to which the exercise is **comprehensive**. What information is gathered, e.g. does the data refer exclusively to one small aspect of the organisation's activities or does it try to capture the totality of the organisation's operations?

- The degree to which the process is **inclusive**. Who is involved in the information gathering process? How far is the information gathered used as part of a process of dialogue and continuous improvement? Are stakeholders invited to offer suggestions for defining performance indicators?

While there are several other measures by which the quality of a social audit should be judged, addressing the issues raised by these three parameters is essential in designing any process of social auditing and reporting.

How is a social audit conducted?

Building on the fundamental concepts outlined above, the following template embraces the major elements of the audit process:

- Define the company's stakeholders – which groups are affected by the company's operations?

- Conduct a process of consultation with stakeholder groups to elicit their perceptions of the organisation's performance and their expectations of what the organisation should stand for.

- Develop benchmarks (qualitative and quantitative) of performance that are relevant to the concerns and aspirations of stakeholders in consultation with them.

- Measure the extent to which these benchmarks are being met.

- Publish the results of both the consultation exercise and the measures of performance. Where possible, comparative benchmark data should be provided to judge the organisation's performance against both internal and external targets. This report should be widely available and incorporate a response mechanism allowing stakeholders to provide feedback and thereby encouraging an ongoing process of dialogue.

- Ensure that the whole process is open to the scrutiny of an external verifier independent of the company.

- Develop a corporate response to the audit process in terms of setting targets for future performance improvements and a commitment to repeating the social audit cycle.

Source: Andrew Wilson, Director, Ashridge Centre for Business and Society, UK

Social Accountability 8000 (SA8000)

Social Accountability 8000 (SA8000), which defines itself as the first, comprehensive global system was devised by a US organisation, the Council for Economic Priorities. It is one of the more successful attempts to develop an auditable standard for third party verification. Large claims are made for SA8000 which, like ISO 9000 (the standard for quality control assurance) and ISO 14000 (on environmental management), is designed to work across countries, across industries and in companies of all sizes. According to the Financial Times, SA8000 provides *"what other initiatives have lacked: a common framework for ethical sourcing".*

SA8000, which at present primarily addresses the manufacturing and consumer goods sectors (footwear, clothes and toys), is based upon the seven core ILO Conventions, which protect rights in the workplace. It includes provisions on child labour and forced labour; it sets down health and safety measures; it guarantees the principles of non-discrimination, freedom of association and the right to collective bargaining as well as protection from physical or mental abuse. It requires companies to respect fair working hours and to offer a living wage. SA 8000 reaffirms the obligation on companies to uphold national laws and to respect other international instruments such as the Universal Declaration of Human Rights and the Convention on the Rights of the Child.

In order to certify a company as being SA8000 compliant, the auditor must be satisfied that there is no area of 'major non-conformance'. But in cases where there are issues of 'minor non-conformance', provided that the company is able to make rapid improvements and carry out any Corrective Action Requests made by the auditor, certification can be granted. After six months the auditor returns for a surveillance visit to assess whether action has been taken.

SA8000's approach is to bring about continuous improvement rather than immediate exclusion of companies. Companies have to demonstrate that they have effective management systems in place to guarantee compliance and they need to keep their performance under constant review. Companies also take steps to bring all their suppliers and sub-contractors in time into line with SA8000. But the real strength of the new approach, according to the Council for Economic Priorities, is the threat of commercial sanctions. Certification will attract customers and offer companies the opportunity to gain a competitive advantage. In this way, SA8000 provides a positive incentive. Instead of companies and countries racing to the bottom to have the lowest wages and standards, they have to compete to raise their standards.

> **Source: Council on Economic Priorities Accreditation Agency (CEPAA), New York, US**

Limitations of SA8000

While SA8000 is a significant landmark in the development of social auditing standards, it has also been the subject of criticism on the part of some NGOs because of the issues which it fails to address:

● SA8000 aims to improve workers' conditions but there is little scope for their active involvement either in defining the standard or in assessing the company's performance.

● There is no obligation on any of the parties to ensure that the workforce or trade unions receive a copy of the auditor's report. The auditors are employed by the company and their professional responsibility is to the management alone.

● There is an absence of any agreement about participation and transparency throughout the process. Although the auditors rely on trade union bodies and NGOs for background data, they are not able to share their findings with the key informants. This hampers the ability of civil society to monitor implementation of the standard or to ascertain whether corrective action has been taken.

● The professional obligations of the auditors may also lead to another conflict of interest. Auditors may observe not only violations of SA8000 but of domestic law as well. Most jurisdictions have prohibitions on forced labour, violations of health and safety regulations and abusive disciplinary practices – even if these are weakly enforced. Yet the auditors do not see it as their duty to report such violations to the appropriate national authorities.

● Certification under SA8000 is designed to be flexible and inclusive but this gives the auditor a wide margin of discretion, which runs the risk of undermining the whole process. For example, the requirement that companies should respect the right of all personnel to form and join trade unions and to bargain collectively has been set aside in the case of China to avoid all suppliers in a key country being denied certification.

● SA8000 does not address the presence or activities of security guards or military personnel directly. Yet in many cases private security personnel and the military have been responsible for serious human rights violations, not simply against the workforce but against members of the wider community.

● SA8000 requires that companies provide an avenue to workers to lodge complaints about the company's implementation of the standards. In practice, there is little evidence of an appeals procedure which is safe and harassment-free.

● The responsibility for implementing SA8000 lies with the individual unit. While Northern retailers are pressuring local suppliers to become certified few are prepared to share the costs.

> **Source: Collection of views expressed by NGOs, including Labour Rights in China and Asia Monitor Resource Center**

AA1000 – a process standard in social and ethical accounting, auditing and reporting

AccountAbility (AA) 1000 is a process standard developed by the Institute of Social and Ethical Accountability, launched in 1999. It is designed to support an organisation's strategic management and operations. It is not a substantive performance standard insofar as it focuses on the processes that an organisation should follow to account for its performance, rather than the level of performance the organisation should achieve. The AA1000 process standard covers the following stages:

• Planning
• Accounting
• Auditing and reporting
• Embedding
• Stakeholder engagement

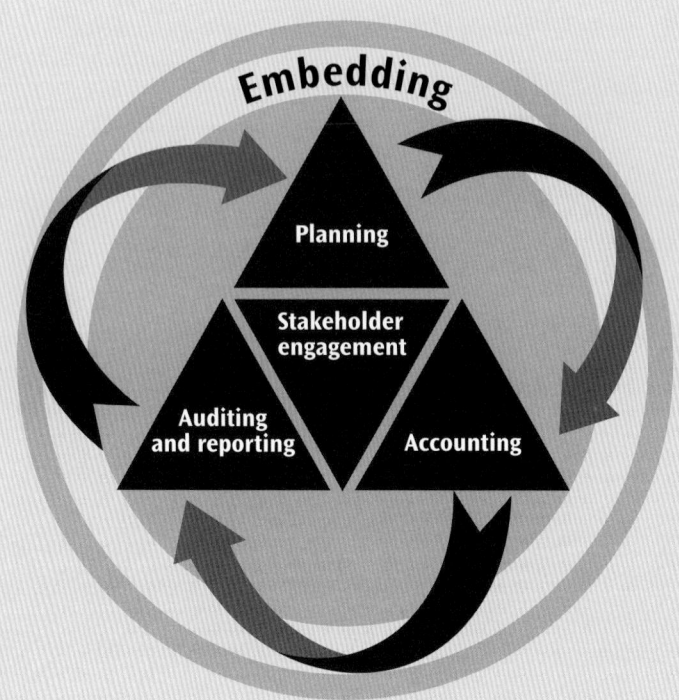

AA1000 is based on a set of principles which should be used in designing and managing the process of reporting. The model can be applied to a company's reporting on its performance with regard to human rights.

Principles relating to the scope of the reporting process:

Inclusivity

Are the view and needs of all stakeholder groups included?

Completeness

Are all the appropriate areas of the company's activity incorporated into the process in an unbiased way?

Materiality

Is all significant information included that might affect the opinion of one or more stakeholder group?

Regularity

Is the process regular, systematic and timely to enable it to support the decision-making of the organisation and its stakeholders?

Principles relating to the credibility and value of the reporting process:

Quality assurance

How accurate and valid are the company's reporting and supporting information systems?

Accessibility

Can each stakeholder group access the material communicated easily and cheaply?

Information quality

Is there **comparability** with the organisation's previous performance, external benchmarks, statutory regulation and other norms?
Is the information **reliable**, allowing stakeholders to be confident that it is free from material error or bias?
Is the information **relevant** to stakeholders?
Is the material **comprehensible** to stakeholders with regard to language, style and format?

Principles which support the management of the reporting process on an ongoing basis:

Embeddedness

Is the process well-integrated into the organisation's operations, systems and policy-making, rather than a one-off exercise to produce a social report?

Continuous improvement

Does the accounting, auditing and reporting process show clear signs of improvement, and are targets being set for the future?

Source: Mike Peirce, Institute of Social and Ethical Accountability, London, UK

4.4 Regulatory pressure

International Labour Organisation conventions

The International Labour Organisation (ILO) is a UN body which is tripartite in its structure, involving governments, trade unions and corporations in the drafting of conventions and recommendations. It was created out of a common desire to ensure that international competition in production and trade took place on the basis of respect for universally acknowledged minimum labour standards. One of the ILO's main functions is to set international standards in the labour and social policy field. These standards, known as Conventions or Recommendations, range from general principles to specific recommendations on particular industries or groups of workers.

ILO conventions, once ratified, create binding obligations on governments. Even in the absence of ratification, they serve as a standard of reference for national law and practice.

In its Declaration on Fundamental Principles and Rights at Work, adopted by the International Labour Conference in June 1998, the ILO stated *"that all Members, even if they have not ratified the Conventions in question, have an obligation arising from the very fact of membership in the Organisation, to respect, to promote and to realize, in good faith and in accordance with the Constitution, the principles concerning the fundamental rights which are the subject of those Conventions, namely:*
a) freedom of association and the effective recognition of the right to collective bargaining;
b) the elimination of all forms of forced or compulsory labour;
c) the effective abolition of child labour;
*d) the elimination of discrimination in respect of employment and occupatio*n.*"*

Governments of member states must report annually to the ILO on what they have done to comply with the Conventions. The ILO has a supervisory system that is intrusive, authoritative and fully independent. The ILO can point to many examples of countries being induced to end violations of human rights proclaimed in the Conventions. Although the ILO's regulatory mechanisms are directly applicable only to governments, ILO conventions carry a strong normative force which is increasingly being transmitted to companies via trade unions, non-governmental organisations, consumers and ethically conscious shareholders. Companies which ignore ILO conventions will find themselves under growing reputational pressure.

There are commonly considered to be seven 'core ILO conventions' which provide the internationally accepted framework for labour standards (see Section 2.5). Companies would be well advised to incorporate these core standards into their human rights policy.

Extension of legal jurisdiction over companies

There has been considerable debate at the World Trade Organisation about the responsibilities of transnational corporations. The reality is that these organisations operating across national boundaries are not liable under international law (including human rights law) because they are not states, although some of them are wealthier and arguably more influential than many states. Nor is it easy for those individuals affected by their actions, such as the Bhopal or Cape victims, to hold them to account under local law as the parent corporation attributes any liability to its local subsidiaries.

On the question of whether it is acceptable for a company to apply standards in its overseas operations which would not be acceptable at home, many transnationals argue that they are simply required to abide by the laws of the countries in which they operate. The opposing view is that it is morally wrong, and should also be unlawful in the jurisdictions where their parent companies are registered, for a transnational to be able to hide behind local laws which it knows will not adequately protect human rights as defined by international instruments. A number of leading TNCs today apply principles of conduct to the totality of their operations.

In November 1999, the UK Court of Appeal decided that 3000 South African asbestos victims suing British multinational Cape Plc should argue their cases in South Africa, rather than in the UK, where the claimants wished to pursue their claims.

Many workers at Cape's factory in Barking, East London, also developed asbestosis but they have been able to utilise the UK Courts to seek compensation. In contrast, it is practically impossible for the South African victims to obtain justice in their local courts due to their inability to obtain funding to bring a claim, fear of persecution, corruption, or because the local subsidiaries are insolvent or uninsured.

The Cape claimants have lodged an appeal with the House of Lords, which if it goes ahead will be of significance to the future of transnational accountability. Alternatively, the case may be referred to the European Court of Justice on an aspect of the 1968 Brussels Convention (an agreement between EU States which regulates jurisdiction and enforcement of judgements). This could result in the UK having to fall into line with the rest of the European Union, where transnationals can be sued in their home courts irrespective of the location of their corporations and the origin of victims.

Whatever the outcome of the Cape case, transnationals will come under growing pressure from human rights lawyers and campaigning bodies to ensure that their worldwide operations comply with international standards, as well as standards applicable within the home countries where they are registered.

Source: Richard Meeran, chairman of Solicitors' Human Rights Group and representative of claimants in the Cape plc case

European Parliament Resolution

In January 1999, the European Parliament passed a resolution by a large majority to create a legally binding framework for regulating European transnational corporations (TNCs) operating in developing countries. If implemented, this will expand the reach of important principles of human rights to TNCs.

The resolution was the product of six months of consultation with NGOs and companies undertaken by Richard Howitt MEP, who was asked by the European Parliament to act as rapporteur. The resolution asks the European Commission and the European Council to create a legal basis for reaching the extra-territorial activity of European TNCs. It envisages that any form of regulation will adopt existing international standards as a starting point, including ILO core standards, OECD Guidelines on Multinational Enterprises and the basic human rights protections embodied in the Universal Declaration of Human Rights. By relying on and combining these existing instruments, a European code of conduct will enhance their legal status and benefit from the extensive jurisprudence already available on these protocols.

The resolution requests the European Commission to set up an independent monitoring body to promote observance of the proposed European code of conduct, identify best practices, and receive complaints about corporate conduct from interested parties. This platform would consist of independent experts in addition to representatives from companies, trade unions and NGOs. Such a body would set an important precedent for expanding the scope of international human rights law to accommodate the growing influence of TNCs. The resolution also recommends that the EU seeks greater accountability of TNCs at the international level – the OECD, the ILO, the World Trade Organisation, and the UN Conference on Trade and Development.

In response to the resolution, as well as to other developments, the European Commission has funded the establishment of a European-wide organisation to promote codes of conduct, their monitoring and verification. Launched in December 1999, the *Institute for Ethical Production and Consumption in Europe* (IEPCE) has set as its first task a number of 'round-table' discussions with industry, trade unions and NGOs in every member state.

The most significant aspect of these developments is that they are indicative of the political will that exists within the EU to ensure that TNCs operate to internationally recognised standards.

Source: Richard Howitt, Member of the European Parliament

Selective purchasing laws

A number of selective purchasing laws have been enacted in the US by state and city governments. Most prevent those state and city governments from dealing with companies doing business in Myanmar because of the human rights situation in that country. The states with selective purchasing laws on Myanmar are Massachusetts and Vermont. Over 20 cities have enacted such laws on Myanmar, starting in 1995 with Berkeley (California), Madison (Wisconsin) and Santa Monica (California), and now including New York City, Los Angeles, Portland, San Francisco and Oakland. Several localities in Australia recently joined the list. And Myanmar is not the only target: Berkeley, Oakland and Alameda County adopted selective purchasing laws on Nigeria during the period of military rule in that country, and Berkeley also targets companies doing business in Tibet if their operations have been criticised by the Tibetan government-in-exile.

Transnational corporations might not have been too worried in 1995 when two college towns and Santa Monica passed these selective purchasing laws, but when the State of Massachusetts and some large cities made the move in 1996 it created a reaction. The corporate anti-sanctions group called USA*Engage started keeping track of state and local selective purchasing laws on its website. The list of states and cities continued to grow longer. University students and others organised boycotts of companies doing business in Myanmar. Meanwhile a number of multinational corporations decided to pull out of Myanmar, including Apple Computer, Philips Electronics, Eastman Kodak, PepsiCo, Atlantic-Richfield, and Hewlett-Packard.

US Secretary of State Madeleine Albright, addressing the National Conference of State Legislatures on 17 April 1998, expressed broad support of selective purchasing laws, saying that she and "President Clinton recognize the authority of state and local officials to determine their own investment and procurement policies, and the right – indeed their responsibility – to take moral considerations into account as they do so."

In November 1998 the federal district court struck down the Massachusetts law as unconstitutional, on the basis that it violates the federal government's power to regulate foreign affairs. The Attorney General of Massachusetts appealed against the ruling. On 22 June 1999 the US Court of Appeals, while agreeing that human rights conditions in Myanmar are "deplorable," upheld the lower court's ruling, finding that the Massachusetts law was unconstitutional on three counts: it interferes with the federal government's foreign policy powers, it impinges upon Congress' powers to regulate foreign trade, and it was pre-empted by the federal sanctions on Myanmar. Massachusetts Attorney General Tom Reilly has asked the US Supreme Court to review the case.

Source: Christopher Avery, Business and Human Rights in a Time of Change, Amnesty International UK

London Stock Exchange requirements for managing risk

A number of committees were set up in the UK in the 1990s to consider ways of improving corporate governance. The most recent of these, chaired by Nigel Turnbull, Finance Director of the Rank Group, was set up by the Institute of Chartered Accountants of England and Wales to come up with proposals for implementing the Combined Code of the Committee on Corporate Governance, which was published in 1998. A key thrust of the Turnbull Committee's recommendations is that companies consider not only narrow financial risks, but all major risks, including those to intangible assets such as their brand and reputation.

The London Stock Exchange has informed all UK listed companies that they will have to implement the Turnbull Committee's recommendation that they take account of "environmental, reputation and business probity issues" when considering internal controls. From 2000 it is a listing requirement of the London Stock Exchange for companies to create systems to identify, evaluate and manage their risks and to make a statement on risk management in their annual report.

The Turnbull Committee's recommendations are important to the human rights agenda because human rights issues often hit companies hardest at the risk management level. There are few things more damaging to a company's reputation than public disclosure of its complicity in the violation of human rights, especially when physical violence is involved. Many companies find themselves operating in close co-operation with governments that have poor human rights records. In such cases, the human rights context of their operations may pose an acute threat to their reputation.

In the context of the Turnbull Committee's recommendations many companies will have to give considerably more attention to identifying their exposure to human rights and exploring how this exposure can be managed. The recommendations outlined elsewhere in this primer may be of use in developing a core framework for good risk management in this area.

4.5 Normative pressure

Codes of Conduct

For companies, internal codes of conduct are a means by which they can implement their business principles. The contexts in which codes of conduct have been introduced into businesses vary. Some are in response to a particularly damaging event and can be seen as a means of preventing similar events re-occurring. The British Airways code *The Way We Do Things – The Code of Business Conduct* was drawn up in the wake of its controversy with a competitor, Virgin Airlines. NatWest's code *It's Good Business* was published following criticism of the behaviour of one of its subsidiaries in a take-over situation known as the Blue Arrow Affair. Other corporations have seen the commercial importance of setting out guidelines for their staff and management on how to respond to situations not covered by existing policies. These codes may be a response to stakeholder pressure that is threatening to damage the company's reputation, even if it is not related directly to any particular incident or crisis.

The purpose of such codes is to set out a basis for business dealings for all employees throughout the world. They enable the company to aspire to consistent practice in all its operations and thus to maintain a reputation for trustworthiness which is crucial to the long-term sustainability of the corporation.

Codes also provide a useful means of drawing attention within the company to existing relevant international standards and human rights instruments, such as ILO conventions. Codes can help clarify what an organisation's responsibilities are – both moral and legal – in situations where national legislation or practice is incompatible with human rights standards.

Stephen Rubin, Chairman of Robert Stephen Holdings Ltd., (the parent company of the Pentland Group plc which owns a range of sportswear and clothing brands) believes codes of conduct help a business:

> *"We cannot have representatives of the company going off in different directions, so we need to resolve 'do we conform to this code, or don't we'? If we do, then we must ensure that we do everything possible to encourage all our employees to conform. As an example, we should bring corporate citizenship into the criteria for annual bonus. If we do not, then there is nothing more for the business to do. Employees may or may not follow the particular set of guidelines, but, from the 'risk aversion' point of view, we must be prepared for an incident from the public, media, customers etc. accusing us of not following best practice, and we should have our reasoning (defence) ready."*

Human rights statements by transnational corporations

The following is a collection of extracts from the policy statements of a selection of transnational corporations which have incorporated explicit support for human rights into their Business Principles or Codes of Conduct:

BP Amoco	

- 'BP Amoco supports the principles set forth in the Universal Declaration of Human Rights...'
- 'Business Unit Leaders are expected to engage in open dialogue and consultation with local communities and their representatives, non-governmental organisations and government at all levels to ensure that potential issues arising from our operations are identified and the risks addressed.'
- 'We will not choose business partners to do things on our behalf which contravene these commitments.'
  What we stand for... Our Business Policies, Commitments and Expectations BP Amoco, Feb 1999

BT	

- 'We are committed to protecting and enhancing the human dignity of all those engaged with our company. To this end we have based our policies and procedures on the principles set out in the United Nations Universal Declaration of Human Rights...'
- 'As the global influence of multinational companies widens, many of the principles enshrined in the Universal Declaration of Human Rights are relevant to the way they conduct themselves.'
- 'We in BT will continue to take human rights issues seriously. We shall seek to apply our commitment to human dignity in whatever part of the world we operate.'
  The Way We Work... Getting it right BT, July 1999

Nokia	
	• Nokia will respect and promote human rights. Nokia recognises with the international community that certain human rights should be considered fundamental and universal. • Among those rights that Nokia views as fundamental and universal are: freedom from any discrimination based on race, colour, sex, language, religion, political or other opinion, national or social origin, property, birth, or other status; freedom from arbitrary detention, execution or torture; freedom of peaceful assembly and association; freedom of thought, conscience and religion; and freedom of opinion and expression. Nokia will not use child or slave labour, or slavery-like conditions or treatment, and not contract with sub-contractors or suppliers who do so. **Code of Conduct** Nokia, 1999

Norsk Hydro	
	Observance of the following [international standards] will be regarded by Norsk Hydro as its *"licence to operate"* in local communities affected by the company's industrial activities. • Norsk Hydro supports the Universal Declaration of Human Rights and will not engage in activities that impair the enjoyment of human rights; • Norsk Hydro will engage in open dialogue and consultation with stakeholders in local communities and elsewhere regarding impacts of company operations; • Norsk Hydro's operations will not endanger the physical safety, security and health of members of communities affected by such operations; • Norsk Hydro will remain neutral in respect of race, religion, gender, age, caste, cultural identity and similar factors; • Norsk Hydro will respect the intrinsic value of diverse cultures and traditions in communities where it operates. **Community Responsibilities attached to Industrial Development** Norsk Hydro, March 1999

Novo Nordisk	
	• The question of human rights relates to virtually all aspects of our business. It is a matter of respecting employees and providing healthy and safe working conditions – the starting point of this report. Human rights are also a question of the way we interact with suppliers, customers, local communities, authorities and other external stakeholders. • We support the United Nations' declaration on human rights. Human rights must be respected and promoted throughout the world. Observing human rights is an important part of conducting our business as responsible citizens. Our approach will seek to align the company with the vision of the United Nations' Universal Declaration of Human Rights in a way that has practical meaning for the way we work. **Engaging society** Novo Nordisk, 1998

Premier Oil	
	• 'Premier recognises human rights issues as part of our business environment. Our human rights policy is a commitment to the fundamental rights pronounced in the Universal Declaration of Human Rights. These rights should be protected and promoted everywhere.' • 'Premier is always willing to enter into dialogue with stakeholders to develop greater understanding of human rights and developmental issues, and also the impacts of our operations. This process will influence the selection of methodologies to benchmark, evaluate and report on our social performance over time. • Premier will develop and implement new procedures at all levels of its business in relation to those human rights that it is able to promote directly in its operations and supply chains.' **The Future is Responsible Business** Premier Oil, November 1999

Rio Tinto	
	• 'The Rio Tinto Group's policy on human rights is based on its support for the United Nations Universal Declaration of Human Rights...' • 'Rio Tinto supports and protects the dignity, well being, and rights of those with whom it is directly involved: its employees and their families, and the local communities which are neighbours of its operations.'

- 'The Group aims to develop ever greater understanding of human rights issues, and of their consequences for its operations. It seeks dialogue with representative bodies, with international and other non-governmental organisations, and with others in the business community. The aim is a practical common effort to promote respect for human rights.'
The Way We Work... our statement of business practice Rio Tinto, Jan 1998

Shell

- 'To respect the human rights of their employees...'
- 'To conduct business as responsible corporate members of society... to express support for fundamental human rights in line with the legitimate role of business...'
Statement of General Business Principles, Shell, 1997

- 'We support the Universal Declaration of Human Rights...'
- 'We speak out in defence of human rights when we feel it is justified to do so.'
- 'We are setting up Social Responsibility Management Systems designed to help in the implementation of our Business Principles and therefore our stated support for human rights.'
- 'We are developing awareness training and management procedures to help resolve human rights dilemmas when they arise. This includes a guide to human rights for managers.'
The Shell Report 1998

Statoil

- Respect for human rights is an integral part of Statoil's corporate values. Our concern for human rights applies throughout all our operations.

We will contribute to improvements by:

- Ensuring that our employees understand the significance of human rights in all our operations;
- Assessing conditions relating to human rights for new and existing projects in the same way as we consider other high-priority aspects such as health, the environment and safety;
- Informing the relevant authorities about Statoil's values, including our policy on human rights, health, the environment and safety;
- Giving preference to partners and suppliers who demonstrate respect for human rights;
- Engaging in dialogue on human rights with international organisations and petroleum-related industry.
Statoil and human rights Statoil, 1998

Can corporate codes of conduct meet the need?

According to Sophia Tickell of Oxfam (GB), codes of conduct can go some way towards ensuring that foreign direct investment has a positive impact on host communities. The very process of companies' consulting on draft codes provides an opportunity for NGOs and trades unions to raise concerns and reflect the perspectives of poorer communities and workers. They also provide a statement of corporate intent that can be monitored against practice. Those codes based on existing human rights architecture, such as the UDHR and ILO core labour standards, help to clarify what a company considers its responsibilities to be – both morally and legally – in situations where national legislation or practice falls short of these international standards.

To be genuinely effective and meaningful, codes of conduct should be drawn up with the following in mind:

- they should be accompanied by independent monitoring and evaluation of their application, which involves the communities or workers directly affected;
- they should not be an excuse to avoid compliance with existing international norms;
- they are not a substitute for effective regulation pertaining to responsible corporate practice.

NGOs, in conjunction with trades unions and community organisations, can contribute to the development of corporate codes on specific issues. The differences in size between companies and NGOs make it extremely difficult for NGOs to undertake meaningful and sustained monitoring or verification on the application of codes, but they can contribute to identifying who on the ground should be involved in such a process.

Source: Sophia Tickell, Policy Adviser, Oxfam GB, UK

Sector-wide and cross-sector initiatives

In addition to individual company codes of conduct, some leading companies are supporting sector-wide and cross-sector initiatives towards improving industry-wide standards. Such initiatives are often undertaken in partnership with NGOs and stakeholders. Companies seek NGO involvement to benefit from their technical knowledge of human rights and development issues, and from the legitimacy that such associations can offer companies. At the same time, NGOs need to be cautious not to be co-opted or compromised by their links with companies, in order to preserve their independence and integrity. The growing collaboration within an industry or sector is due, in part, to an increasing awareness that a human rights scandal hitting one company in the sector is likely to subject the entire sector to greater public scrutiny. It has been a common response to consumer concerns in developed countries about working conditions under which consumer goods are produced; eg. carpets, toys, footballs, clothes and trainers.

The **World Federation of Sporting Goods Industry** (WFSGI) brings together companies which are prepared to collaborate to promote best practice across the industry, underpinned by a model code of conduct. Companies can show a corporate leadership through supporting the principles of such initiatives. By acting collectively, companies are sending strong messages to suppliers, governments, consumers and other stakeholders, that certain issues, such as labour rights, are non-competitive, and of common concern. WFSGI has played an active role in seeking to eliminate the problem of child labour through its Action Plan for Child Labour (1996), its Sialkot Programme in Pakistan, and and other collaborative initiatives.

www.wfsgi.org

Dr Gill Seyfang, of the Overseas Development Group at the University of East Anglia claims there is a major problem with the proliferation of codes, both internal and external. In her view, they lack consistency of wording and coverage, and in many cases do not include the core ILO conventions. The codes drawn up by corporations tend to respond to issues which arouse the greatest concern in western consumers' minds (such as the use of child labour), but to neglect other issues which do not generate such media attention, for example, the right to form unions and bargain collectively, or the needs of vulnerable groups of workers such as homeworkers.

The Ethical Trading Initiative – helping companies improve their human rights policies and practices

The Ethical Trading Initiative (ETI) is an alliance of mainly retail or consumer goods' companies, NGOs and trade unions operating in the UK, whose aim is to improve labour conditions in the global supply chains which produce goods for the UK market. The desire to improve labour conditions reflects a concern for basic human rights and an acknowledgement that there is room for improvement in the adoption and implementation of codes of conduct that reflect internationally agreed standards.

The ETI was formed by key individuals in the above sectors who wanted to determine whether a co-operative approach to improving labour conditions in the supply chain could be taken. This was seen as an alternative to an adversarial approach based on campaigns and boycotts on one side, and company resistance on the other. ETI is funded by membership fees paid by its member organisations and by a grant from the UK Government's Department for International Development which has backed this project from the outset.

ETI has drawn up a nine-point Base Code setting the following standards: no forced labour; freedom of association and the right to collective bargaining; safe and hygienic working conditions; no use of child labour; payment of a living wage; limits to working hours; no discrimination; regularity of employment; no harsh or inhumane treatment. The Code can be found in full on ETI's website (www.ethicaltrade.org in English, Spanish and French). This Base Code reflects the core conventions of the International Labour Organisation, which is the pre-eminent authority in global labour standards.

By joining ETI, companies have the opportunity to participate in cross-sector pilot projects and to benefit from the shared learning about practical ways of improving human rights in the workplace.

Source: Dan Rees, Manager ETI Secretariat, London, UK

Sainsbury's participation in the Ethical Trading Initiative

Sainsbury's, a major UK food retailer, was one of the founder members of the Ethical Trading Initiative. The company has participated in a number of ETI schemes aimed at piloting codes of conduct within its supply chain. The suppliers targeted have included producers in Zimbabwe, wine growers in South Africa and banana plantations in Costa Rica.

Sainsbury's joined ETI because it had become apparent over time that the subject of ethical trading was a growing area of concern for their customers and for the public at large. The company established its code of conduct early in 1998, issuing it to all its own brand suppliers in March of that year. Following this, it began to carry out visits as a way of raising awareness of its code of practice and of the associated issues relating to socially responsible trading. It also started to explore opportunities for independent monitoring of compliance with the principles set out in the code, by working with a number of third party auditing companies.

The visits to suppliers formed an important base for learning in the light of the problems encountered over implementation of the code. For example, language barriers can hinder the flow of information or can present opportunities for misinterpretation. It is essential to have a knowledge of local culture, customs and laws in order to make sensible judgements relating to compliance with certain sections of the code of practice. A lot of the issues identified are not particular to Sainsbury's but apply to any company attempting to monitor its suppliers.

The ETI acts as a forum to discuss issues encountered during such visits. It is an excellent mechanism for exchanging information, learning from mistakes and sharing best practice. In addition, it helps with the identification of suitable bodies within specific countries that might provide local information and advice. Being a cross-sectoral initiative, the ETI provides Sainsbury's with the opportunity to work with trade unions and other organisations with appropriate expertise. This makes it easier to develop suitable standards and identify effective processes for monitoring and verification.

Finally, ETI membership has provided Sainsbury's with the opportunity to benchmark its activities against those of other companies. It has also provided the means to help translate genuine customer concerns into a practical action plan for improved standards of ethical trading across its worldwide supplier base.

Source: Geoff Spriegel, Director Technical Divison, Sainsburys, UK

In the case of labour rights, Seyfang's research shows that the most effective codes of conduct are those drawn up by firms in collaboration with workers' organisations (not just the traditional trades unions, but also women workers' associations), as well as development organisations campaigning for improved working conditions. These are typically based on the core ILO conventions as a bare minimum, usually including independent monitoring procedures for greater credibility.

Fair Labour Association

The Fair Labour Association (FLA) is a US-based non-profit organisation aimed at protecting the rights of apparel and footwear workers worldwide. The FLA grew out of the Apparel Industry Partnership (AIP), a voluntary initiative supported by the White House in 1996, which brought together a group of manufacturers, human rights, labour rights and consumer organisations to address labour rights violations in the apparel and footwear industries.

The FLA will oversee the enforcement of a sector-wide code of conduct and monitoring principles drawn up by the AIP in 1997. The Workplace Code of Conduct addresses labour issues in nine key areas: child labour, forced labour, discrimination, harassment, freedom of association, wages, health and safety, hours of work and overtime compensation. These broadly reflect labour standards covered in the core ILO convention, although no explicit reference is made to any universal standard.

To date, ten companies have agreed to participate in the process: Adidas-Solomon AG, Kathie Lee Gifford, Levi Strauss & Co., Liz Claiborne inc., L.L. Bean, Nicole Miller, Nike, Patagonia, Phillips Van Heusen, and Reebok. In addition, 121 colleges and universities have affiliated with FLA, requiring their licencees to comply with FLA standards. Four public interest organisations have participated in the setting up of the FLA; the International Labour Rights Fund, the Lawyers' Committee for Human Rights, the National Consumers' League and the Robert F. Kennedy Centre for Human Rights.

The FLA Charter Agreement creates a 'first of a kind' industry-wide code of conduct and monitoring system. The agreement lays an important foundation for the creation of a credible, independent monitoring system that will hold companies publicly accountable for their labour practices, as well as those of their principal contractors and suppliers around the world. The FLA will accredit independent monitors, determine whether companies are in compliance with the Association's standards, and issue public reports that will assure consumers that they are purchasing apparel and footwear that has not been made under exploitative conditions.

Critics believe the FLA model does not go far enough in pressing for greater public accountability of business. However, certain NGOs argue the scheme has potential for bringing about more responsible conduct among companies. *"We believe it is a useful first step in what will be a dynamic process to improve continually means of enforcing worker rights,"* says Justine Nolan, manager of the business and human rights programme at the Lawyers' Committee for Human Rights in New York. Ms. Nolan adds, *"We view the FLA as a creative and innovative approach to promoting dialogue between the human rights community and business, with the aim of promoting workers' rights in the global marketplace. It provides a mechanism for moving beyond the traditional exposure of the human rights community to create a real means of enforcement."*

Sources: www.lchr.org/sweatshop/main.htm; and Justine Nolan, the Lawyers' Committee for Human Rights, New York, US

Global Sullivan Principles

Another call to business to uphold human rights and good corporate citizenship and governance comes in the form of The Global Sullivan Principles, launched in 1999. Originally devised as principles for companies operating in apartheid South Africa, the Reverend Leon Sullivan has expanded them to embrace the global operations of transnationals. Individual companies are invited to sign up to the principles, thereby publicly affirming their commitment to the universal standards indicated therein. However, the Sullivan Principles do not make explicit reference to the existing UN human rights architecture, such as the Universal Declaration of Human Rights and ILO labour conventions. A company adopting these principles should not view them as an alternative to the adoption of internationally established human rights instruments.

Objectives

- to support economic, social and political justice by companies where they do business;
- to support human rights and to encourage equal opportunity at all levels of employment, including racial and gender diversity on decision making committees and boards;
- to train and advance disadvantaged workers for technical, supervisory and management opportunities;
- to assist with greater tolerance and understanding among peoples; thereby, helping to improve the quality of life for communities, workers and children with dignity and equality.

For further information, see US State Dept. website (www.usis.it/wireless/wf991101)

The OECD Guidelines for Multinational Enterprises

The OECD Guidelines for Multinational Enterprises (MNEs) are recommendations to companies made by the governments of OECD member countries. They are part of the Declaration on International Investment and Multinational Enterprises, adopted by the governments of OECD member countries in 1976. They are currently undergoing a process of revision. Their aim is to ensure that MNEs operate in harmony with the policies of the countries where they operate. These standards cover the full range of MNE's operations and deal with issues such as information disclosure, competition, taxation, employment, industrial relations, and environment. The human rights context of the OECD Guidelines is contained largely in the chapter on Employment and Industrial Relations. Companies are encouraged to:

- respect the right of their employees to be represented by trade unions and other *bona fide* organisations and engage in constructive negotiations with them on employment conditions;
- provide assistance and information to employee representatives;
- provide information for a true and fair view of the performance of the enterprise;
- refrain from discriminatory practices in their employment policies;
- not exercise unfair influence over *bona fide* negotiations with employees' representatives.

By providing a common frame of reference, the guidelines have contributed to the process of building confidence and predictability between companies, labour and governments. The OECD has established an institutional framework for promoting the guidelines, handling enquiries and assisting in solving problems which may arise between business and labour in matters covered by the Guidelines. The non-binding nature of the guidelines and the lack of monitoring and verification mechanisms are seen as weaknesses by the NGO community which is pressing for the revised guidelines to incorporate a stronger implementation framework.

UN Global Compact

The United Nations has added its voice to the many calls to business for an active commitment to corporate responsibility and respect for human rights. At the World Economic Forum in Davos in January 1999, Kofi Annan presented companies with a challenge to join the UN in 'a global compact of shared values and principles which will give a human face to the global market.' "Specifically I call on you – individually through your firms, and collectively through your business associations – to embrace, support and enact a core set of values in the areas of human rights, labour standards, and environmental practices." While in no way legally binding, Kofi Annan's call to companies to play their part in upholding universal rights adds yet more momentum and authority to the debate on business and human rights.

Of the nine principles Annan laid out, six refer to human rights, including labour rights, and three to the environment. The first six are as follows:

1. Businesses should support and respect the protection of internationally proclaimed human rights; and
2. make sure they are not complicit in human rights abuses
3. Businesses should uphold the freedom of association and the effective recognition of the right to collective bargaining;
4. the elimination of all forms of forced and compulsory labour;
5. the effective abolition of child labour; and
6. eliminate discrimination in respect of employment and occupation.

The UN Office of the High Commissioner for Human Rights is charged with engaging the private sector in pursuit of the first two principles, and the ILO with the last four principles. A Global Compact website has been developed with the help of companies, business associations, UN partner agencies and NGOs to bring together information on the Compact's three areas. It also highlights various tools and resources to assist business leaders in translating the Global Compact principles into corporate mission statements and management practices.

The Global Compact website:
- makes the case for business commitment to human rights, labour standards and environmental issues
- provides companies with managerial tools, such as good practice examples and case studies as well as an environmental impact checklist and matrices for documentation of stakeholder interactions
- links business and civil society users with organisations worldwide which are involved with related issues, and keeps them up-to-date on new initiatives in the corporate citizenship field
- regularly updates a calendar of related events, within and outside the UN system;
- circulates articles, reviews and position papers drawn from newspapers, journals, UN publications, the Internet, academic debate and corporate and organisational statements.
- integrates UN data bases on labour, human rights and the environment.

Source: www. unglobalcompact.org and www.unhchr.ch

An embarrassment of riches?

The landscape for companies approaching the question of human rights is becoming increasingly crowded with ever more principles and guidelines. While this is proof that human rights is being pushed more and more onto the corporate radar screen, the profusion of different guidelines for companies can prove confusing. The Universal Declaration of Human Rights and the ILO core conventions provide the best and most internationally accepted framework of human rights standards.

The Confederation of Norwegian Business and Industry has broken new ground as a business association by compiling a checklist for companies addressing human rights against specific articles of the UDHR. Companies may find it helpful to consider some of the points raised, as they develop their own human rights strategy. The text appears in Part III.

2 Case studies

HUMAN RIGHTS – is it any of your business?

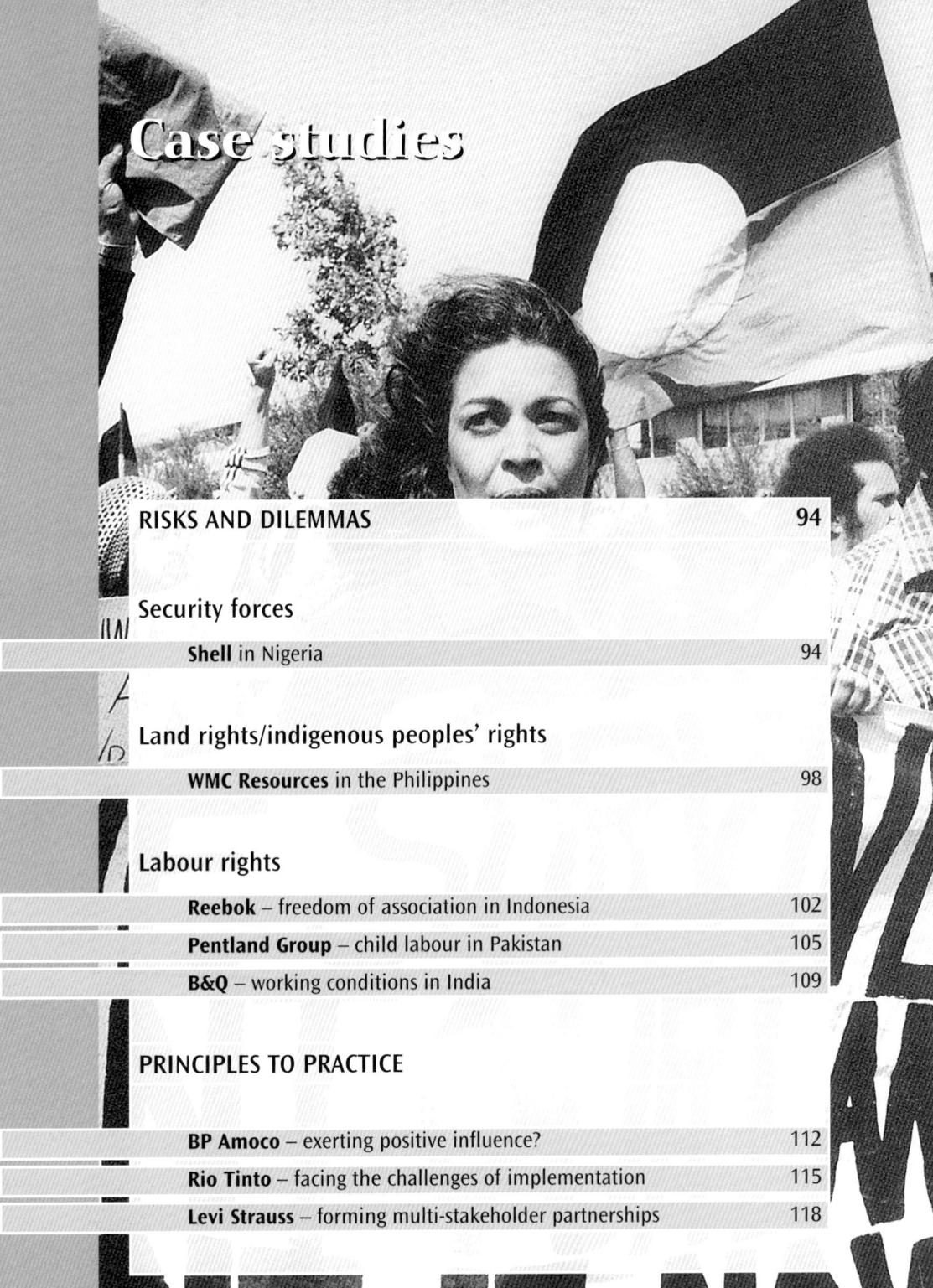

Case studies

Risks and dilemmas

The following case studies, referred to in Section 2, explore how various TNCs have tackled particular human rights challenges. While every situation is particular to a specific context, there are useful lessons to be drawn for other companies facing similar challenges.

Shell – Linking security to human rights in Nigeria

"Addressing human rights abuses calls for action at many levels from political will and high policy, to 'bearing witness' and practical actions by companies and others. Our job is to work out what realistically we can do to enhance human rights in the context of doing our business – and then do it."

Robin Aram, Vice President of External Relations & Policy Development, Shell

For many years, people living in the Niger Delta have endured violations of their civil and political rights by the Nigerian security forces. While inter-ethnic conflicts and demands by minority groups for autonomous recognition have been at the heart of some conflict in the Delta, the overlay of oil production and inequities in the distribution of the proceeds have exacerbated tensions. The widely held perception amongst communities within oil producing areas is that they have suffered adverse social and environmental consequences of oil production, while realising none of the benefits.

The absence of a visible government presence within the Delta has led to oil companies – Shell in particular – becoming the focus of discontent and sometimes violent protest. The often heavy handed responses of the State's security forces has prompted concerns internationally, most notably following the judicial execution of Ken Saro-Wiwa in November 1995. Securing the safety of employees and company assets while respecting human rights is one of the main challenges facing Shell in Nigeria, given the social and political context of its operations.

Background

Since Nigerian independence in 1960, the allocation of oil revenues has been a source of political debate and conflict. In principle, a proportion of the government's oil revenues is returned to the producing states and communities, which has fuelled campaigns for the creation of new states. In practice, much of the funds either fail to reach the producing areas or are distributed through patronage to extract political benefits. Widespread corruption has further diluted the development potential of oil revenues.

The Shell Petroleum Development Company (SPDC), a joint venture[1] operated by Shell, is responsible for 40% of Nigeria's total output and 55% of onshore production. Its infrastructure comprises 6,200 km of pipelines and flowlines, 86 flowstations and the Bonny and Forcados oil terminals. Much of the infrastructure dates from the early 1970s and is in the process of being renewed.[2] Since 1989, on average 221 oil spills have been recorded each year. Half the spills result from corroding pipework (accounting for 27% of the volume spilled). A further 28% are attributed to sabotage (accounting for 60% of oil spilled) – a figure strongly contested by communities in oil-producing areas.

Although compensation for damages related to oil spills is one of the only means whereby communities derive 'benefits' from oil revenues, communities claim that compensation never reflects the value of their loss. Each oil spill is investigated by a team comprising members of the affected communities, government environmental agencies and SPDC. Where sabotage is proven to be the cause of spills, no compensation is paid on the basis that to do so creates an incentive for sabotage. However, Bronwen Manby of Human Rights Watch concluded from several visits to the Delta that *"sabotage is often carried out by contractors that stand to benefit from clean-up contracts rather than by the individuals whose land is affected".* The murky issue of sabotage and its causes is further clouded by the capacity of affected communities to benefit from clean-up related employment.

Protest, persecution and security

In the 1990s, protests relating to oil production, linked to environmental damages and the failure of local people to realise economic benefits, escalated in the Delta region. One of the most notorious incidents occurred at a Shell facility at Umuechem in October 1990, when 80 unarmed demonstrators were killed and hundreds of houses burned by the Mobile Police – a notorious

---

1. The partners are Nigerian National Petroleum Corporation (55%), Shell (30%), Elf (10%) and Agip (5%). 2. This infrastructure became due for renewal and upgrade in the mid-1980s, when the government owned 80% of the joint venture and its income from oil had fallen by two thirds from a 1981 peak. The government was unwilling to commit adequate funds to upgrading – and it was only in 1992 that SPDC received approval to commit $100 million per annum. In the meantime corrosion had become a significant problem.

paramilitary force linked to numerous abuses of human rights. A judicial commission of enquiry concluded that the mobile police had displayed *'a reckless disregard for lives and property.'*[3]

In the early 1990s, the Movement for the Survival of the Ogoni People (MOSOP) campaigned for a greater share of oil revenues, political autonomy and ownership of the oil beneath their land. It demanded $6 billion in rent and royalties from Shell and compensation of $4 billion for environmental degradation. MOSOP also accused Shell of colluding with the government in the genocide of the Ogonis. Faced with increasing intimidation, Shell withdrew from Ogoni land in early 1993. The execution in November 1995 of nine MOSOP leaders attracted widespread international condemnation. It also led many advocacy NGOs to call for a boycott of Shell to hold it accountable for *'environmental abuses and tolerance of injustice'.*[4]

Human Rights Watch has catalogued a depressing cycle of protest and repression in the Delta.[5] These include alleged instances of harassment, unlawful detentions, beatings, torture and killings. These actions are often prompted by demands for compensation following oil spills, or protests. International concerns at human rights infringements in Nigeria have also been raised in various reports and resolutions of the UN's Human Rights Committee. The focus of protest and repression has recently shifted from Ogoni-land to the territory occupied by the Ijaw people, the fourth largest ethnic group in Nigeria. This follows the issue of the Kaiama Declaration by an Ijaw Youth Conference in December 1998, calling for the withdrawal of the Nigerian military and oil companies.

And yet Shell and other oil companies have a legitimate interest in providing a secure environment for employees, and in protecting oil infrastructure. Hostage-taking of oil workers is on the increase in the Delta – during a six-month period in 1999 there were 50 kidnappings of Shell employees or contractors and 150 Shell facilities were occupied, shut-down or otherwise disrupted.[6] The perpetrators are mainly disaffected groups of youths demanding jobs, compensation or development assistance. For Shell, striking a balance between providing security to its employees and protecting human rights has proved to be difficult, particularly since security is primarily the responsibility of the State's security forces.

Shell's policy on human rights & security

In early 1996, Shell embarked on a major consultative exercise known as "Societies changing expectations". Prompted in part by public reaction to the Brent Spar incident and allegations of complicit involvement in human rights abuses in Nigeria, human rights emerged as one of the key concerns of those consulted. This led to a revision of the Shell General Business Principles, which now explicitly commit Shell to *'respect the human rights of their employees'* and *'express support for fundamental human rights in line with the legitimate role of business'*. In 1998, the company produced a management primer on Business and Human Rights.

Shell also engaged with a range of stakeholders such as Amnesty International and Human Rights Watch regarding the security aspects of their Nigerian operations starting in 1996. This led to a revision of Shell's rules of engagement with the state security forces – the police and the military – to accommodate the *UN Basic Principles on the Use of Force and Firearms* and the *UN Code of Conduct for Law Enforcement Officials*. The experience in Nigeria has prompted a broader-based review of security provision, and the

development and adoption in 1998 of group-wide *Use of Force Guidelines*. These provide for inter alia seeking assurances from state forces that the use of force will respect human dignity and peoples rights, will be proportional to the threat, will minimise damage and injury, and advising them that they will be held accountable for any excessive use of force.

All Shell security personnel are to receive adequate training in operating procedures that are consistent with relevant codes of conduct. The guidelines stipulate the 'rules of engagement' for calling in or contracting with state security forces. They also provide advice on acceptable courses of action and responses against those who represent a threat to the security or safety of personnel or company assets.

Security in the Niger Delta
In Nigeria, Shell has a legal obligation to call in the forces of law and order in situations where people or property are at risk, yet it has publicly committed to not hiding behind a military shield. The emphasis is on passive preventative security, which avoids the need to use force. The *Use of Force Guidelines* and associated procedures feature in the training Shell provides to the Nigerian Police detachment assigned to protecting SPDC's assets. Shell reserves the right to screen and reject police based on their possible involvement in human rights abuses. Its current rules of engagement are discussed with other state security forces in their areas of operation, as are the conditions under which security forces will be called in.

Following the events at Umuechem, Shell adopted a policy of not calling in the Mobile Police in response to security threats. Their guidelines today specifically state that *'under no circumstances must SPDC engage or call to be engaged any military or paramilitary force, e.g. Mobile Police'*.

Shell – Linking security to human rights in Nigeria

3. The Price of Oil: Corporate Responsibility and Human Rights Violations in Nigeria's Oil Producing Communities. Human Rights Watch, 1999. 4. Cited in the US-based Sierra Club's call for a boycott. 5. The Price of Oil, Human Rights Watch, 1999. 6. John Vidal, Guardian, 15/09/99.

Shell's policy is not to use force or request its use to suppress peaceful demonstrations, even if production is disrupted. Although some apparently peaceful demonstrations lead to acts of violence, for the most part Shell chooses to evacuate personnel from sites under threat, rather than risk confrontations that could lead to human rights abuses.

In recent years, Shell has become more active in its efforts to promote human rights in the Delta. For example, after the arrest of Batom Mittee and others during the January 1998 Ogoni day celebrations, Shell appealed for the highest standards of human rights to be upheld. It also lobbied the government for the withdrawal of the Mobile Police from Ogoni land in the interests of creating an atmosphere conducive to reconciliation. Batom Mittee was subsequently released and the Mobile Police withdrawn. Gerry Matthews, External Affairs Adviser to Shell, is careful not to claim credit for these positive developments. *"It does, however, illustrate that local managers feel empowered and are committed to taking a public position on these issues"*.

One aspect of Shell's 'security provision' that has recently attracted criticism is the employment of local people to patrol flowlines, rights of way, flowstations, etc. to alert Shell to unsafe situations, such as broken fencing around well installations. While initially seen as providing much needed employment to local people, as unemployment in the Delta has spiralled the divisions between employed and unemployed have sparked local tensions. This has prompted demands for employment, sometimes based on extortion, which can be hard for local managers to resist. While allocating this work to non-locals would relieve tensions between local people, it would also exacerbate the underlying causes. Alan Detheridge, Senior Corporate Advisor to

Shell, says *"the answer ultimately lies in a more equitable allocation of oil revenues to stimulate social and economic development within the Delta"*. Shell has engaged in dialogue with the Nigerian Government on the question of revenue allocation and is encouraged by the current administration's commitment to addressing this issue.

Human development as a route to security

Shell recognises the need to improve stability within the Niger Delta if the current security situation is to improve. The ongoing programmes for renovation of faulty infrastructure plays a small but important part of this strategy. More importantly, the people in the Delta need to become beneficiaries from oil production – rather than its casualties.

Despite the wealth created from oil production, the Niger Delta remains impoverished. Per capita GNP is below the estimated national average of US$ 280.[7] The mosaic of creeks and swamps make travel and infrastructure development difficult in much of the region. Illiteracy rates are high and health and educational provisions are poor. Shell has invested US$33m per annum in community development initiatives in the past five years, primarily on healthcare and education. However, local critics claim that the development impact is limited, as much of the money is siphoned off by corrupt officials and contractors, resulting in substandard facilities. They also claim that Shell's social investment is aimed at 'buying favours' and has been divisive.

While Shell rejects such claims, it has recently shifted its community investment strategy to one driven by participatory appraisals of the needs of communities, with a strong emphasis on community participation. The aims are to increase family incomes through

support to micro-enterprises and improved access to credit, and to improve welfare through enhanced health, education and agricultural services. In this respect they are also working collaboratively with the NGO Living Earth on a number of pilot projects, which aim to demonstrate the benefits of working with communities in a more participatory manner. But if suspicions of patronage in the allocation of community development support are to be overcome, Shell needs to find alternative mechanisms for providing assistance to communities.

Human Rights Watch has recommended that the oil companies operating in the Delta pool development resources, both to maximise the potential development impact and to avoid charges of patronage. While Shell is broadly supportive of the suggestion, a spokesman suggested that it has *"attracted limited support as the interests of the other oil companies differ somewhat"*. Another NGO representative cast a different light on the issue of collaboration: *"There is a sense that Shell has broken ranks with some of the other oil companies by being proactive in the human rights arena… they are uneasy about going down the same route"*. In the meantime, Shell has sought to develop partnerships with development NGOs and local communities. It has also publicly declared its support for reallocating more revenues to oil producing areas to provide increased financial support to human and economic development.

Conclusion

There is an emerging consensus that for peace and stability to be restored to the Niger Delta, the communities must view themselves as net beneficiaries from oil production. Achieving that shift in perspective is no easy task, given the legacy of past failures by

---

7. World Bank, World Development Indicators 1999

governments, persecution by security forces, inter-ethnic rivalries, and the sense that oil companies have put profits before principles. Shell believes that it has a contribution to make towards helping change perceptions. This includes a responsibility to continue to demonstrate support for human rights. Whether or not communities finally come to see themselves as beneficiaries depends not only on Shell, but also crucially on the Nigerian government and on the ethnic groups living in the Delta.

The case of Shell in the Niger Delta illustrates the extent to which the social and economic development of local communities and the level of state repression are inextricably linked to the security of company personnel and installations.

Shell – Linking security to human rights in Nigeria

WMC – Learning to respect indigenous land rights

> A Bla'an cannot sell his land. He cannot cut himself off from the land. The Spirit of the land and the Spirit of the forest cannot be given away."
>
> **Anteng Frey, Bla'an Traditional Leader**

A defining characteristic of many indigenous peoples is their close attachment to ancestral lands and a perspective on land 'ownership' that differs markedly from western concepts. The Bla'an communities of the highland areas near Mount Matutum on the Island of Mindanao in the Philippines are no exception. Their ancestral lands in part coincide with an area of low-grade copper mineralisation, the Tampakaen Copper Project, which the Australian-based minerals development company WMC Resources Ltd. (formerly Western Mining Corporation) is looking to develop. Respecting the fundamental rights of indigenous peoples in line with its policy commitment has been central to WMC's approach to the exploration work at Tampakaen.

Yet some critics of the project allege that WMC has been underhand in its dealings with indigenous peoples. In particular, NGO concerns centre on whether informed consent has been obtained from indigenous communities to enable mining to proceed, or whether their rights are being infringed. WMC's experience at Tampakaen provides some valuable insights into how companies can avoid a 'clash of cultures' and develop relationships of mutual respect with indigenous peoples.

Background

In 1995, WMC and the Philippine Government entered into a Financial or Technical Assistance Agreement (FTAA) to explore for and develop mineral deposits on the Island of Mindanao. The FTAA originally applied to a 90,000 hectare block of land, which must be progressively reduced over five years to less than 5000 hectares.[8] The potential minerals development area must be contained in this 5000 hectares.

The focus of WMC's exploration activities is home to some 2,300 people belonging to five indigenous Bla'an communities. The animistic polygamous Bla'an have traditionally engaged in hunting and slash and burn agriculture, practices that are still prevalent in the highland areas around Mount Matutum. In lowland areas, the distinctive culture of the Bla'an has been largely immersed by Christian settlers from the Visayan Islands in the central Philippines.

Land tenure and broken promises

Prior to WMC commencing exploration at Tampakaen, none of the Bla'an communities had legal title to the lands they occupied. The Bla'an do not recognise land 'ownership' in the western sense, but instead see themselves as custodians of their traditional lands. Bla'an custom recognises the spiritual beings who inhabit the earth and the sky as the true owners of this land. As custodians, they enjoy certain rights such as occupancy, hunting or the right to cultivate. Custom prevents the Bla'an from alienating the land by selling it, but permits leasing of land to 'outsiders'. This might include other Bla'an from outside a village cluster or Visayan immigrants.

Leasing between Bla'an group members has generally been for a specified time period, whereupon the land reverts to the traditional owner. Cross-cultural leasing of land (to Visayan or Muslim settlers) has been at the root of many land disputes and encroachment onto traditional Bla'an areas. In some instances, non-Bla'an believed they had bought leased land and were understandably unwilling to relinquish it. In others, non-Bla'an lessees have knowingly exploited their occupancy of leased land to obtain a Certificate of Occupancy from the Government (in effect legal title).

During the Marcos administration, the allocation of logging concessions on Bla'an traditional lands without reference to the Bla'an led to conflict between the Bla'an and the military, who were deployed to secure access to lands. The history of the Bla'an interaction with logging companies is one punctuated by broken promises. Some Bla'an formed armed groups to combat the military, and their successful resistance led to an amnesty being issued for the Bla'an during the Aquino Presidency. WMC has had to contend with the Bla'an deep-seated mistrust of outsiders – the legacy of progressive encroachment by Visayan settlers and logging companies.

Assistance with ancestral domain claims

Under the terms of its FTAA with the Philippine Government, WMC is obliged to "recognise and respect the rights, customs and traditions of indigenous tribal peoples". This is broadly consistent with the Indigenous Peoples Policy that WMC adopted in 1995—the first policy produced by a mining company that committed to developing relationships of mutual understanding and respect with indigenous peoples.

Consultations with tribal leaders during the early stages of exploration highlighted the protection of traditional lands and securing legal title as the primary concerns of the Bla'an. *"The highland Bla'an have seen their lowland counterparts become*

---

8. WMC had reduced the FTAA to 44,000 hectares by November 1999.

dispossessed of their traditional territories and disenfranchised, with a resulting breakdown in traditional culture", says Stephen Davis, formerly Group Geographer at WMC. *"They see securing their traditional lands as essential to maintaining their cultural integrity."* The 1987 Constitution in principle provides for 'ancestral domain for indigenous cultural communities'. Such communities may assert claims for association with ancestral lands to the Department of Environment and Natural Resources (DENR), in order to obtain a Certificate of Ancestral Domain.

But the process of identifying boundaries, collating evidence to support claims and documenting the necessary information was beyond the resources and capacity of the illiterate Bla'an. WMC and the five indigenous Bla'an communities in the proposed minerals development area signed 'Heads of Agreement' in 1994 and 1995, in which the company committed itself to supporting their ancestral domain claims. Over the next two years, detailed ethnographic and archaeological records were prepared and the boundaries of traditional territories were mapped. Reports compiling the work in support of the ancestral domain claims were submitted to the Government by four of the five Bla'an communities. To date, four have been awarded Certificates of Ancestral Domain, which recognise their rights to occupy and use the land.

Mutual benefits of certification

While a Certificate of Ancestral Domain does not confer legal title to the land, it helps to secure improved tenure over traditional lands and provides a foundation for community development. Having obtained certificates, the communities are obliged to develop resource management plans for their areas. Without certification the Bla'an are

technically illegal squatters on much of the land they occupy [9] – land that in the past has been intruded upon and occupied by others without legal obstacles – resulting in conflict. Certification prohibits occupation by unauthorised people, thereby reducing the potential for conflict.

For WMC, aside from its obligations under the FTAA and its own indigenous peoples policy, there was also a business case for its work with the Bla'an communities. For example, it was important to determine which communities were potentially affected by its operations and the boundaries of their land to comply with certain provisions of the 1995 Mining Act. WMC also sees benefits in the improved stability associated with the Certificates of Ancestral Domain Claim, in helping to reduce the risks relating to any agreement it may reach with the communities.

But there are some dissenting voices. The relationship between WMC and one of the five Bla'an communities has soured since the signing of the Heads of Agreement and the company is no longer permitted to enter their lands. WMC accepts their position. A number of Australian-based NGOs and church groups have been most vocal in their criticism of WMC. One critic remarked; *"There is not much mutuality here… all we see in Tampakaen is deception and intimidation"*. This perspective is strongly rejected by the company, which points to its continued licence to operate from most communities.

While acknowledging the potential value of WMC's work with communities to obtain Certificates of Ancestral Domain Claim, some NGOs are critical of its motivations and question whether the communities concerned appreciated that it represents a step towards ceding control of the land to WMC. The company's response is that its work was offered unconditionally,

and that Bla'an communities are now empowered to make informed judgements about their future development.

Moving towards formal agreements

Consultations initially focussed on the Bla'an Tribal Councils by virtue of their proximity to the potential minerals development area. WMC's recognition of the Bla'an's ancestral lands and support for Certification caused some resentment amongst Visayan settlers, as it is seen as constraining access to 'unoccupied' lands. Similarly, the initial focus of community development initiatives was in highland Bla'an communities. To redress these imbalances, WMC extended its consultation and community development assistance to non-Bla'an Village *(barangay)* Councils and Municipal Councils in the wider project area. Its aim has been to sign formal 'Principal Agreements' with the five Bla'an indigenous communities, three municipalities, five barangays and individual landowners in the potential minerals development area. *"Shifting the focus from just the Bla'an to be more inclusive has not totally removed resentment"* says Gavan Collery, WMC's Manager of Corporate Affairs, *"but it has allowed WMC and the communities to progress in what we want to achieve for mutual benefit".*

The agreements contain obligations on both WMC and communities. Under the Mining Act of 1995, WMC is required to pay a one percent royalty on gross output to *'a trust fund for the socio-economic well being'* of affected indigenous communities. It also mandates a contribution of 1% of mining and milling costs to social and infrastructure development to affected barangays, although WMC has undertaken to contribute the larger sum of 1% of gross output. The Principal Agreements establish the basis for compensating for any disturbance or relocation consistent

WMC – Learning to respect indigenous land rights

---

9. Land with a slope greater than 18% is classified as public land that can not be disposed of by the Philippine Government. This includes much of the land in the project area.

with World Bank guidelines [10] (although no relocation has taken place to date and the expectation is that less than 50 households will need to be moved if the project proceeds).

In return, communities are required inter alia to give irrevocable consent to WMC having access to lands, conducting mining, and to agree not to support or promote action or conduct which would threaten financial arrangements made by WMC in relation to the mine. The agreement does, however, not preclude the community from participating in the project approval process: *"The community may, notwithstanding any other provision of this Agreement ... participate in the public consultation process associated with the grant of that (Environmental Compliance) Certificate without any restraint under this Agreement."* This provision gives the community a say in the approvals process.

The signing of Principal Agreements is perhaps the most controversial aspect of WMC's engagement with the Bla'an. The 1997 Indigenous Peoples' Rights Act [11] requires companies to obtain the 'free and informed consent' of indigenous peoples for exploration and mining. The question of whether informed consent was given at Tampakaen is central to the concerns of WMC's critics, and more broadly to negotiations between companies and predominantly illiterate indigenous peoples. That the signing of the Principal Agreements unlocks immediate developmental financial assistance is also of concern.

The company argues that all reasonable efforts were made to develop an informed understanding amongst communities of the implications of mining. For example, three-dimensional models were used to illustrate the changes that mining will bring during community consultations. Similarly, a number of tribal and local

government leaders have been flown to visit a similar mine operated by Newmont Mining in Sulawesi, to experience large-scale mining at first hand. The company developed a detailed 'execution protocol' to provide internal assurances that the various stages towards achieving free and informed consent have been adhered to. For example, staff have to sign-off in detail to the effect that consultations have been initiated, information has been provided in local languages, key participants have attended meetings (that are taped and subsequently minuted for approval), etc.. On occasions, the WMC Project Manager has refused to sign off on the initial approvals process as his staff did not provide sufficient evidence of adequate consultation in line with the protocol. But some NGOs still question whether the indigenous communities have a truly informed understanding of the potential adverse social and environmental impacts that large-scale mining can bring.

Community Development Initiatives

The FTAA obliges WMC to help *'develop the host and neighbouring communities of the contract area'.* In advance of the signing of Principal Agreements and in consultation with communities, WMC has provided funding for community development priorities such as schools, clinics and advice on making the transition from slash and burn agriculture to sedentary and more sustainable agriculture. The latter responds to the difficulties of limited access to remaining land resources. WMC also has been assisting reforestation of previously logged areas. On average, 15% of WMC's annual budget has been spent directly on community development (A\$ 6.3m/US\$ 4m in total).

Security concerns

In the past, there have been NGO allegations of military harassment of indigenous communities at the behest

of WMC. The military periodically visit the area, which is reportedly frequented by insurgent groups, illegal loggers, and marijuana growers. In one incident, it was incorrectly alleged that the Philippines Military attacked a Bla'an village within WMC's FTAA to persuade them to relocate (despite the village in question lying several kilometres outside WMC's potential minerals development area). Yet the presence of security forces in the areas has posed a dilemma for the company with respect to its approach to security provision.

Elsewhere in the Philippines, it is common practice for the military to secure access to lands on behalf of companies. To its credit, WMC has consistently resisted any military involvement in obtaining such access or security provision at Tampakaen. Its policy has been that it would be unable to obtain the support of communities or achieve its business objectives by relying on a military force to provide security. The relatively low-key security presence around its facilities indicates that WMC may be having some success in gaining the confidence of local communitites, and that on balance, WMC may be on the path to earning a local licence to operate.

Conclusion

The juxtaposition of minerals and indigenous communities inevitably leads to controversies when a proposal emerges to develop a mining operation. Determining whether a company has managed to balance commercial and community interests is always difficult, particularly when the starting point for many detractors is that all mining is inherently damaging to the rights of indigenous peoples and their environment.

At Tampakaen, WMC has helped indigenous communities to secure Certificates of Ancestral Domain Claim,

---

10. World Bank Operational Directive 4.30: Involuntary Resettlement. 11. In late 1997 the Philippines Government passed the Indigenous Peoples' Rights Act, which confers ownership of sub-surface natural resources on indigenous communities. This contradicts the State's declared ownership of sub-surface resources in the Philippines constitution, and clarification is being sought through the courts.

which they might not otherwise have obtained in a fairly short time-frame. They have attempted to develop a relationship of mutual benefit with indigenous communities and to ensure that lasting community benefits remain, even if the project does not proceed. They have also respected the choice of one Bla'an community to deny them access to their lands. Finally, they have taken steps to develop an informed understanding amongst communities of the implications of mining. Whether they have succeeded may only emerge if the project is ultimately developed by WMC.

Note: On 8 February 2000, WMC announced that following a review of its expenditure programme, the company had decided to withdraw from its project in Cuba, the Philippines and Uzbekistan because the projects do not meet the company's current investment criteria. This decision includes the Tampakaen project.

WMC – Learning to respect indigenous land rights

Reebok – Setting an example for freedom of association?

Reebok International Ltd, a US-based leading worldwide designer, marketer and distributor of sports, fitness and casual footwear, apparel and equipment. It has a projected annual revenue of approximately $2.5 billion in 1999. Its major brands are Reebok, Rockport, Greg Norman and Polo Sport Footwear. It has some two dozen footwear contractors and several hundred apparel contractors. Reebok employs 6,000 people and there are over 100,000 workers involved in making Reebok products. The initial focus of its human rights work has been on Reebok brand footwear which accounts for over 80% of its turnover.

Reebok is unusual in that it has accepted the principles of freedom of association and collective bargaining and in selected ways is seeking to implement them (and other standards) through a model of worker empowerment. As the Calvert Group, the leading US socially responsible investment company, notes: "Reebok International is one of the very few companies in the US footwear and apparel industry that has shown a consistent public commitment to improving its practice. Compared with its industry peers, Reebok has been quicker to respond to claims of worker abuse". This case study focuses on the corporation's policy and practice on worker empowerment and its relationship to the right to associate and engage in collective bargaining.

Some civil society activists argue that empowerment cannot address problems caused by gross imbalances of power. Reebok has focused its initiatives, according to Doug Cahn, company Vice President for Human Rights, on "strengthening worker-management relations and strengthening legitimate trade union activity through the facilitation of training". In some instances (see below) it has also sought to influence the environment in which it operates.

Reebok's starting point

Encouraged by the strong personal views of its CEO, Paul Fireman, Reebok has had a long history of a corporate commitment to human rights issues. This corporate culture led Reebok to ask how it could operationalise its human rights values within its own core business. One catalyst was when US President Carter sent Mr Fireman a copy of the new Levi Strauss 'Terms of Engagement' in 1992 as an example of good corporate practice. Levi Strauss' informal benchmarking process provided a focus for Reebok's own thinking and led to the development of its 'Human Rights Production Standards'.

Advancing staff understanding

Reebok has progressed from a short checklist of items focusing on health and safety and wage issues to a 40-page booklet to help managers interpret and implement the company's guidelines. This evolution of understanding is the result of, and reflected by the growth of, the Human Rights Production Standards department. From two people based in the corporate

headquarters in 1992, the team today consists of twelve people, three of whom are in North America and the rest based in Latin America and Asia. This evolution within the company is mirrored by a similar process within its subcontractors. Sharon Cohen, Vice President for Public Affairs, recounts that when they first sent their code to their suppliers in 1992 and indicated that they wanted to visit the factories, the most common response from the suppliers was to claim that they were already meeting the requirements. Factory visits by Reebok staff showed this often not to be the case.

Communications and empowerment

Reebok's code is unusual in that it includes an explicit reference not only to freedom of association but also to the right to collective bargaining. Reebok has in many instances chosen to define the operational opportunity and challenge of implementing these rights in terms of achieving better communication with workers and achieving greater levels of empowerment.

Introducing a Worker Communication System

Reebok launched its Worker Communication System in 1997 in order to provide workers with a secure system to express workplace concerns in a manner which allowed Reebok and factory management to focus on specific issues at the time they came up. An early and critical step was to ensure factory managers would not harass workers for contacting Reebok and that a manager would not participate in an investigation of a complaint if he/she was the subject of that complaint. Part of the challenge was to get workers to understand how the system worked (e.g. the fact that they could be anonymous) and to be confident that there would no negative repercussions from using such a system. This involved large posters explaining the process in the local language,[12] drop boxes in areas where workers felt safe to use them (e.g. even in toilets) and printed pre-paid mailers with telephone numbers for emergency use.

Reebok have taken the unusual step of making available the number of complaints received from workers:

12. WCS materials have been translated into Mandarin, Thai, Indonesian and Vietnamese.

Categories	CS	CN	TH	IN	VN	Total
Discrimination	1	13	0	1	3	18
Working Hours/Overtime	98	111	51	19	8	287
Factory Rules/Regulations	39	10	55	36	13	153
Wages	42	177	151	80	31	481
Freedom of Association	0	0	3	0	2	5
Health & Safety	148	45	25	23	19	260
Interpersonal Relations	110	111	36	14	35	306
Other	159	188	53	72	25	497
Totals by country	**597**	**655**	**374**	**245**	**136**	**2007**

Complaints registered, October 1998 – September 1999

CS: China South   **CN: China North**   **IN: Indonesia**   **TH: Thailand**   **VN: Vietnam**

Whilst being an important management tool, these figures reflect factors other than whether or not there is a problem in a given factory. For example, Reebok has noted that the number of received complaints relates to the response mechanism (e.g. pre-paid mailers are more popular than drop boxes) and the demonstration of genuine business intent (e.g. the number of complaints goes up when the mailer is accompanied with some training about how it can be used and when management displays the complaint in an anonymous way together with management's response).

The Worker Communication System is not a panacea – it can be very labour intensive and is probably best suited to addressing problems that Reebok might not otherwise hear about. According to Jill Tucker, Reebok's Director, Human Rights Programs for Asia: *"Our long-term goal is for factories to take responsibility for soliciting and responding to worker complaints. For this to happen, factory managers must perceive the value of this system. Some have."*

Since the end of the Suharto era in Indonesia, Reebok has told workers that they should raise the issues with their union representatives and only refer the problem to Reebok if the unions are unable to solve it, so empowering unions to act as the legitimate representatives of workers and ensuring Reebok staff do not play roles for which they are not suited.

Protecting the welfare of union representatives

Aware that freedom of association and the right to collective bargaining are only possible if union representatives are able to perform their role, Reebok has consciously chosen to seek to ensure that these workers are not harassed or discriminated against and has facilitated the development of leadership capacity amongst union activists. At the factory floor level this can mean, according to Ms Cohen: *"We track known union leaders to see that they aren't being discriminated against. Union leaders are often formally designated or we know of them through our contacts with NGOs, churches, etc. So if we do payroll checks and find all have gone, we will follow up."*

Speaking out when the need demands

The issue of whether and how a company can comment on human rights violations is a controversial issue. According to Ms Cohen the answer is to recognise that: *"Companies are influencing government all the time. We can do it for the better or the worse. It might be at a cocktail party or at a formal review when the Ministry of Labour asks us about our five-year plans or through some kind of coalition of multinationals in that country. Often you don't know what you can do unless you try".*

This point is reinforced by Tim Noonan, Head of Education and Campaigns at the International Confederation of Free

Trade Unions: *"We know of local employers in Indonesia who have an open mind about allowing freedom of association and collective bargaining but they are told by their international customers, if you allow unions into the workplace, we will cancel the contract. It is incumbent on multinationals to act within international law."*

One recent and high profile example of Reebok's willingness to push the boundaries was its public appeal to the then President of Indonesia, Habibie, to release the prominent labour rights activist, Dita Sari. In his letter, CEO Paul Fireman said: *"Dita Sari has been particularly effective at raising issues on behalf of factory workers, and her voice deserves to be heard."* Sari acknowledges that Reebok was a unique corporate voice, but that it was the international campaign as a whole that mattered, and this campaign was led by unions, NGOs and human rights activists. Ms Sari notes the irony that just one month before her arrest, she had led a demonstration to Parliament involving 5000 workers from one of Reebok's main suppliers. Accepting that Reebok gained credibility and goodwill from their actions she adds: *"If they are nice to human and labour rights activists, they must also be nice to their workers".*

Helping to develop capacity

Reebok operates in many countries where independent unions are not permitted, such as China and Vietnam. Worker representatives are faced with a complex task when it comes to representing the interests of workers in countries where there is no culture of democracy. In an innovative approach, Reebok has facilitated a pilot training programme that was undertaken by the American Centre for International Labour Solidarity (ACILS). This training was made available to workers selected by all the unions in Reebok factories including SPSI (Serikat Pekerja Seluruh Indonesia, the only union recognised by the Suharto administration) and some independent unions. Reebok ensured that the participants were allowed time off work for two intensive and interactive four-day training sessions, and were not punished in any way for participation. Such innovative partnerships are not easy work – indeed the project is now on hold as Reebok and ACILS review lessons learned.

Using independent verification to ensure continuous improvement

In order to maximise the credibility of its work, and hence the reputational benefit, Reebok chose to work with a local and credible independent social development organisation, rather than opting for a local office of a multinational auditor. Insan Hitawasana Sejahtera (IHS) is an Indonesian social science research and consultancy unit which has a well-established reputation especially in the issues of labour rights and gender. IHS organised a rigorous survey of workers at the two main production factories in Indonesia using female Indonesian interviewers.

Noting that *"unions in both factories were learning how to operate independently of the government in the post-Suharto era"* the audit revealed that SPSI represents about 95% of the workers in each factory, that 70% of workers thought they received positive benefits from membership but *"did not necessarily know the specific benefits"* and only 23% of workers (in one factory) and 2% (in the other factory) had ever attended a meeting. The study highlights the value and possibility of a 'new management culture' in the period of *reformasi*, and notes that individuals and companies are gaining greater awareness of democratic and human rights issues.

Integrating values within the company and down the supply chain

Reebok illustrates the value of having an integrated system with multiple levels of leadership on the issue of human rights. To have a serious impact on factory managers on the ground, the company has recognised the need for commitment from the top which is translated through the co-ordinated work of the supply chain managers and monitoring team. According to Vice-President Cahn: *"You can't do it without the buy-in of the CEO, good credible monitors, and a sourcing team that understand the importance of these issues."*

Future challenges

According to both Cohen and Cahn, the key to success is to: *"Arrange your sourcing structure so that you have maximum leverage. If you are only purchasing a small percentage of a factory's output, it's obvious that you are not going to have so much influence."* Cahn advises that these discussions about human rights, and especially the most sensitive ones such as freedom of association and the right to collective bargaining, are best had at the start of a relationship, alongside discussions on quality, price and turn-around time. Progress has been incremental, starting by introducing a code to suppliers, then bringing in Reebok monitors, and now establishing independent verification.

Reebok's intent is clear from both its code and its implementation activities, both of which go further than many other multinationals in this sensitive arena. Even so, it does not yet claim to ensure full freedom of association and right to collective bargaining throughout its supply chain. However, by listening to the views of local and international stakeholders and by testing innovative options with a high degree of transparency, it is demonstrating how

corporations can begin to take their share of responsibility for what Reebok openly acknowledges is a fundamental liberty. Cahn is, however, clear that: *"Freedom of association is going to be one of the most difficult issues in the future as global brands attempt to find appropriate ways to respect the rights of workers while not getting over involved in the process of negotiations between workers and the managers / owners of the factories"*. In Cohen's view, looking at the sector as a whole, *"at the present time, codes are something that management use. The next step is to get workers to see the code as something they can use – but responsibly, if there is not going to be a downside."*

This essential linkage between codes, worker empowerment and freedom of association is reinforced by Neil Kearney, General Secretary of the International Textile Garment Leather Workers Federation (ITGLWF) who says: *"Codes are not an end in themselves. They are not a substitute for effective labour legislation, nor are they an alternative to workers organising themselves into unions. They will not on their own lead to better wages and working conditions. Even when observed, they cannot replace the representative function of trade unions at the workplace, nor do they cover all the legitimate concerns of workers. They are, however, a useful tool for promoting organising and advancing the bargaining process. The aim should be to achieve a situation where workers and plant management can, as much as possible, resolve problems at local level and negotiate an agreement that enables workers to live reasonably, while not putting in jeopardy the future of the enterprise"*.

Pentland Group plc– Dealing with child labour

Pentland Group plc, a UK-based company with a turnover of £533 million in 1998 owns a number of brands in the sportswear and clothing sectors, such as Speedo, Ellesse and Mitre. It also services a number of 'own label' footwear and clothing companies. It has operations in Europe, North America, Asia and Australia. The focus of this case study is on child labour in the production of footballs in Pakistan.

PENTLAND GROUP PLC

Catalysts for change

● Organised outside pressure

Child labour in Pakistan is a well known phenomenon and in recent years there have been a number of initiatives to address the problem. The issue, however, came to a head when a report from the Lahore-based Human Rights Commission in 1995 documented the scale of the problem. This report acknowledged that the worst problems were in the tanning, surgical equipment and carpet sectors. However, it was the sportswear sector that attracted most international attention. An international campaign was initiated by the trade union movement with the support of some US-based human rights NGOs. Their focus on the football sector reflected this sector's vulnerability to consumer pressure and an assessment that this sector provided the best starting point for a process of wider economic and social development in the region.

The alliance succeeded in persuading an important intermediary organisation – Federation Internationale de Football Associations (FIFA) – to incorporate core labour standards into its licensing agreements. That, combined with a high profile debate linked to the 1996 World Cup, put the international spotlight on the problem. Although the debate was complex and often polarised between local producers and global brands, in particular US brands, it provided the catalyst for a significant gearing up of Pentland's work on child labour.

● Dilemmas

Faced with high-profile pressure, international brand-owners had – in principle at least – the option of terminating contracts with any suppliers who might be using child labour. Pentland rejected this option for several reasons. As a supplier of quality footballs, it could not shift its production to China, as did a number of US companies which were supplying the budget end of the market. Indeed, given questions about labour standards in China, Pentland did not see this option as offering any meaningful reassurance. Moreover, having invested considerable resources in developing relationships in the Sialkot region of Pakistan, Pentland felt a business and moral obligation not simply to walk away.

Their resolve had been strengthened by the situation in Bangladesh in 1993-4 when, faced with a possible US boycott because of their use of child labour, Bangladeshi manufacturers laid off some 50,000 children, thousands of whom are thought to have fallen through the inadequate safety net into less well paid and even more dangerous forms of work including domestic service, breaking rocks, brick making, street vending and prostitution[13] Learning from this experience, Pentland along with some other major brand names decided to take a 'constructive engagement' approach, seeking to work with the factory owners to bring standards to an acceptable level within a reasonable time period.

Key elements of Pentland's approach

● Forming an international alliance

Pentland worked with other members of the World Federation of Sporting Goods Industry (WFSGI) to form a highly unusual alliance (the Atlanta Alliance) involving industry associations, UN bodies (including the International Labour Organisation and UNICEF) and NGOs. This leadership role was made possible by the fact that Pentland's Chairman, Stephen Rubin, was also President of the WFSGI and had recently established an Ethics and Fair Trade Committee; *"We speak for over 10,000 members in a large number of different countries and, when there are problems, can help individuals show that they are conforming to best practice, or help them to achieve it."* This work was initiated under the umbrella of the ILO's International Programme for the Elimination of Child Labour (IPEC). The alliance agreed that the issue of child labour was best dealt with by *"a considered programme in co-operation with local employers and child welfare agencies, focusing on the best interest of the children concerned".*[14] The agreement, signed in Atlanta, focused on two programmes of work: workplace prevention/monitoring and social protection/ rehabilitation.

● Gaining local ownership

Although much of the initial momentum came from international organisations and associations, their focus from the outset was on local ownership. The alliance grew by international players bringing in their

---

13. Rachel Marcus, "Child labour and socially responsible business" in Small Enterprise Development, Vol. 9, No 3, September 1998, pp4-13.
14. From Pentland Group Human Rights and Environment Rights brochure.

local counterparts. Thus, the multinational companies brought in their major suppliers in the form of the Sialkot Chamber of Commerce (SCCI), the ILO brought in monitoring specialists as well as a local NGO, and UNICEF and Save the Children Fund UK (SCF UK) began to encourage the development of local NGO capacity. This approach to building local ownership was a deliberate strategy. According to Lesley Roberts, Business Standards Manager of the Pentland Group: *"Our buyer is over there for a total of perhaps four weeks a year. We are very fortunate because our buyer has developed relationships over many years, but even so we have a limited ability to know what is happening, let alone make sure that things are done differently all year round."*

A key part of Pentland's role has been to keep its local suppliers motivated about participating in the programme and sharing monitoring information with the ILO. This is not a one-off task and is possibly the most critical challenge to ensure a sustainable approach.

● Setting up formal stitching centres – and dealing with unintended consequences

One early agreement between brand-owners and local manufacturers was to move work to formal stitching centres where management could be sure that minimum health and safety conditions were being met and that child labour was excluded. This was and still is a controversial decision since much of the stitching done in the football industry in Sialkot was by women homeworkers, (up to 58%, according to a study by SCF UK), and represents an important source of family income and empowerment. Some women have been excluded from work as a result of this change, though numbers are contested. The advocates of stitching centres argue that without such a move, child labour could not be

eliminated and that the reason for the industry setting up with decentralised labour was, in part, to prevent unions and government bodies ensuring that basic labour standards were met. Those who oppose such centres argue that it has resulted in unnecessary social hardship, especially for women who have been displaced in the process. Some creative problem-solving approaches are being tested (e.g. women-only stitching centres) but it is not clear whether this will prove to be an adequate response.

● Maintain a dialogue – even with opponents

One key player in the debate, the trade union movement, was not formally involved in the Atlanta alliance. Opinions differ sharply as to why. Some believe it was because some key multinationals and local business owners, historically distrustful of unions and smarting from the international campaign, had made it clear that they would not participate if the unions were involved. Others suggest that the unions in Pakistan did not have a large presence in Sialkot and/or a capacity to deal with child labour issues in this sector. However, Pentland continued to maintain informal contact at staff operative levels with the international trade union movement. A senior international union official acknowledged that this helped to some extent to ensure that the unions have broadly supported the project.

● Expect pressures to widen the focus and broaden the alliance

Pressure has been mounting for a more active and transparent involvement of unions. The local union, All Pakistan Federation of Labour, has now opened an office in Sialkot. As homeworkers (including children) are replaced by factory workers, there seems to be a growing push for freedom of association and the right to collective bargaining. Whether and how local and international businesses will be able to

deal with such an evolution of the project remains to be answered. What is clear is that the union movement does not accept that the problem of child labour can be addressed out of context of other issues such as freedom of association and collective bargaining. If unions cannot raise these issues privately from inside the alliance, they have indicated their readiness to do so publicly from outside.

Leadership

Outside pressure has been applied to many sportswear organisations by consumer groups and NGOs. Some of them have started to respond constructively, while others have yet to do so. What allowed Pentland to be an early mover? Part of the answer is that Pentland's Chairman, Stephen Rubin, has a strong personal conviction that *"we need to do the right thing, not the expedient thing".*

● Commitment to implementing a human rights strategy

In a move followed by competitors some years later, he employed a senior NGO professional with a strong background in labour rights and development to head the company's Business Standards department. The primary responsibility for integrating the company's human rights strategy into its operations sits in this unit, with full support of the Chairman. The bulk of the department's workload is taken up in trouble-shooting, using problems to leverage change and responding to opportunities. The strategy is emerging from many actions which are taken one by one but which, over time, create a coherent pattern. Sharing experiences with other companies facing similar challenges underpins this process.

● Leadership through partnership

Pentland has put considerable leadership effort into developing alliances, where there is a convergence of objectives. For example, the company has played an important role in initiating the UK's Ethical Trading Initiative (ETI, see Section 4.5). According to Roberts, *"ETI and projects like it are absolutely essential in getting a more developmental, sustainable response. If you ask one factory or one company to go too far ahead of its competitors, it will become non-competitive. We need ETI and similar projects to allow us to talk to our competitors about things we shouldn't be competing over."*

Pentland is also playing a leadership role in other multi-stakeholder projects including:

- A joint venture on health and safety aspects of chemicals in footwear factories in Vietnam. The Vietnam footwear project is coordinated by the Prince of Wales Business Leaders Forum in collaboration with Pentland, Adidas and Nike, and supported by the UK Government's Department for International Development. This is the first project in Vietnam to bring together major footwear competitors, key Vietnamese ministries, state agencies, international NGOs to ensure cross-sector participation in the initiative. Pentland's role focuses on convening, facilitating and providing leadership, sharing good practice, training materials and financial resources.
- A project in India focusing on the football sector.
- A project in Portugal focusing on homeworkers.

Tools and training

● An expanded risk management approach

Human rights issues such as child labour are an integral part of Pentland's risk management approach. The Business Standards department works with the companies' key suppliers to identify, assess and control the risk associated with production. The programme aims to develop management systems to enable

suppliers to prevent and to respond to problems. Pentland is clear that they can never absolutely guarantee that children are not involved right down the supply chain in the leather-tanning or cotton-growing processes. The key challenge is to focus on the areas of greatest risk within Pentland's sphere of influence.

● Modularised induction and 'hand holding' at a distance

Pentland is in the process of issuing all its buyers with clear and practical guidelines for how to deal with the issue of child labour. This is one of eight modules. The guidelines are extremely practical and very clear. Starting from the desired goals (e.g. *"The factory manager knows the local law concerning young workers"*), the buyer is prompted to ask questions which should allow him/her make an appropriate judgement (e.g. *"Is the factory manager able to give you a brief summary of child labour law? Is he/she correct?"*). The guidelines then suggest what the buyer can do (e.g. *"Provide factory manager with Pentland's summary of child labour law in that country and on next visit ensure factory manager does understand the law"*). Other modules cover topics such as health and safety, worker wages and hours, and homeworkers.

● Decision-making tools

The Business Standards Department uses a simple three-part framework for trying to create strategic alignment in a complex situation: *"Is it good for the community? Is it good for the producer? Is it good for us?"* Underpinning the framework is a commitment to work with factories based on a continuous improvement approach. The company recognises that to limit sourcing to model factories is to exclude other factories from the opportunity of raising their standards of production.

Pentland is currently developing a process for defining how senior

managers will be held accountable for making progress on implementing social aspects into sourcing decisions. Such a system will be important, not least because of plans to link incentive payments with such assessments. Although still to be tested, this could be one way to link work of the Business Standards department into core business strategy decisions.

Future challenges?

How effective has the collaborative approach to tackling the problem of child labour in Pakistan been? Initiatives like Sialkot take considerable senior management time and resources. By 1999, 55 manufacturers have paid $221,000 to the ILO for external monitoring over two years. There are no estimates available for how much manufacturers and multinationals have invested in the stitching centres, internal monitoring systems and provision of education and health services for their workers. SICA and FIFA have also contributed $200,000 over two years and the UK Government's Department for International Development a further £965,000.[15] Whilst the Sialkot project may be the best compromise under the prevailing circumstances – the project has reduced child labour, withdrawn children from inappropriate working situations and provided education to some 6,000 children in the last two years – some observers question the cost effectiveness of this kind of approach for future projects.

By creating well monitored stitching facilities, the project increasingly ensures child-labour-free production, which has resulted in removal of the threat of a boycott. But key questions persist. How suitable is this project as a model for preventing and phasing out child labour in a socially responsible manner in a situation where there are inadequate positive alternatives? Since the football stitching programme was established, the ILO has started

15. Figures from SCF (UK) and ILO-IPEC

Pentland Group plc– Dealing with child labour

programmes to deal with child labour in the surgical equipment and carpet manufacturing sectors. Can this collaborative approach be used as a model for a broader range of labour rights issues in an increasingly competitive market-place?

The ideal solution would seem to be a more preventative approach which deals with the problem before major conflicts arise, based on trust, well-established relationships and reliable self-monitoring, rather than intensive and expensive verification. The corporate sector needs to build in more effective early-warning systems, viewing external pressure as a useful catalyst for change. It also needs to engage in more systematic institution-building with governments to raise local standards in factories across the relevant sector.

B&Q – Addressing working conditions

B&Q is a UK-based DIY manufacturer and retailer with a turnover of £1.96 billion in 1998. It has building, decorative, electrical and hardware product lines, many of which are made in the informal sector or in cottage industry units in developing countries. This case study focuses on B&Q's work with Indian suppliers of such products.

B&Q

Health and Safety as an entry point to labour rights

The initial drive to address Health and Safety (H&S) conditions came in the early 1990s from within B&Q, with its managers taking a strategic decision to extend the scope of its environmental audit to cover H&S conditions. In 1992 B&Q staff visited two brassware factories in India to assess systematically the situation in the knowledge that standards were not likely to be good. As part of the documentation process, the staff took photos to show the human impact of the situation (e.g. a man pouring molten brass not wearing any shoes or other safety equipment). This helped bring home a remote situation to UK-based staff and gain the commitment of the Chairman and Board throughout the process.

Alan Knight, B&Q' Environmental Coordinator, readily acknowledges that H&S is the "very best" entry point for wider concerns: *"There are no cultural values involved. No one can justify cutting off a limb or serious burns on the basis of culture. It fits with the obvious case that a tidier and cleaner factory is a more efficient and productive one. It's also very visual – you can't help but agree even if you don't speak the same language. We have been moving from child labour to health & safety protection, to health and wellbeing promotion, and now to the 'invisible' human rights such as minimum wages and workers organising themselves."*

The growing debate on ethical trade shaped the evolution of B&Q's thinking. The expansion from H&S issues to what B&Q calls 'invisible rights' (e.g. fair wages, the right to associate) is a result of contact with a range of governmental and non-governmental actors. B&Q also found it useful to encourage consultants and NGO partners to be pragmatic in identifying problems and solutions. For example, detailed work by B&Q's NGO partner showed that the beaters and spinners who were involved in rug manufacture had very poor financial security. With advice from the International Resource for Fairer Trade (IRFT), B&Q made a judgement that these individuals were too far down a supply chain, with too many intermediaries, for the company to be able to exert influence through direct contractual relationships. With IRFT's active assistance, B&Q have set up a micro-credit saving scheme, providing the seed capital to get it off the ground.

Key elements of the project

● Taking responsibility

On the basis of previous experience of environmental problems, B&Q adopted a policy of not supporting boycotts of Indian suppliers without first trying to resolve the problem. The company made a similar policy decision in dealing with social issues. Aware that this approach could not work with a very broad supply base, B&Q decided to consolidate contracts with a supplier whom it considered most likely to take the required action. B&Q's initial approach was to bring in some UK-based Health & Safety consultants and its HQ environmental team, working independently of the company's buyers.

● Avoiding the temptation to micro-manage from HQ

This approach delivered significant improvements in H & S standards but was not a sustainable model for moving forward. The buyers kept rotating, which led to a loss of interest and momentum. As B&Q's understanding of the supply chain grew, it became clear that the factory was just the tip of the supply chain iceberg, with a whole cottage industry feeding the factory. Many of the most dangerous H&S risks were outside the factory. Moreover, the ethical trading debate was bringing more issues on to the table (e.g. fair wages). Finally, B&Q was increasing the number of products sourced in India and simply could not engage with each and every factory in this intensive manner using outside experts who were not familiar with local norms and options.

● Thinking globally but forming local partnerships

The Environment Team realised they needed local partners, in part because they needed local expertise and in part because they needed to keep down costs. B&Q used the networks of a respected UK-based international fair trade organisation, Traidcraft, to find an Indian NGO with which they could work. The partner they choose was IRFT. According to Traidcraft's International Director, Andy Redfern, IRFT was one of very few organisations that had expertise in providing wide-ranging support to small fair-trade producers and thus could relate to the situation in the cottage industry sector. relationship succeed.

● Pushing the boundaries in their partnerships

In many ways it might have been easier for B&Q to find the local offices of an international auditor or consultancy, but B&Q recognised that the skills that they really required would not come from this sector. B&Q needed an organisation that could talk both to the cottage industry workers in their own language and also to the factory managers. Initially the factory managers were suspicious of an NGO but with reassurance from B&Q, trust was built. Whilst IFRT were not as easy to 'control' as commercial consultants, they offered B&Q a much-needed competence, which encouraged the company to invest in the relationship.

● Making tough decisions not to buck the market

B&Q soon found that it was not commercially viable to be perfectly 'ethical'. The first supplier met B&Q's requirements in terms of H&S standards but could not, despite efforts all round, match the quality and price that other suppliers could offer. Sticking with that producer could eventually have threatened the product line altogether and would also have raised questions about the business sense of the social standards strategy. So Knight accepted the buyer's recommendation that they switch to a new supplier. This has been done in a way which minimised any adverse PR impact on the first supplier. Knight and his team have built their credibility within the company by making these kinds of tough decisions, which has enabled them to stand their ground on other substantive issues.

● Building ownership

B&Q's strategy has been to put enormous effort into persuading the suppliers and factory owners to take primary responsibility for solving the production problems. As the committed retail partner, B&Q's role has worked hard at convincing factory owners and middlemen of the business benefits of adhering to international standards. The hope is that the factory's standards are raised over the long-term beyond the duration of the relationship with B&Q.

● Leadership

B&Q have had two important sources of leadership. Managing Director Martin Toogood has made clear his personal commitment and engagement by actively participating in training events and visiting suppliers to look at working conditions. Perhaps most importantly, he has empowered the Environmental Policy Controller to *"become the messenger that people would almost like to shoot – but they know they had better not."* Underpinning the entire process of change is the hard-hitting commercial argument that decent working conditions are good for business, and as such should be considered as part of the mainstream business agenda.

B&Q invested in a major training event, with top management present, which brought together all their buyers and suppliers. The purpose was to encourage the suppliers to see that management was serious about the question of standards and to demonstrate that B&Q would work with suppliers to achieve these standards.

Tools

QUEST – an integrated environmental, social and quality audit tool

In 1995 B&Q replaced their *'Supplier Environmental Audit'* with an integrated tool, Quality, Ethics and SafeTy (QUEST), merging their environmental and quality control departments and involving buyers in the process. One of the items on which suppliers are now graded is working conditions. The supplier can be graded from A – E (see box). B&Q have set themselves the target that all suppliers will at least reach grade B. Moreover, they have also reported their baseline assessment of their supply chain.

QUEST Principles on working conditions in developing countries

Grade A: The supplier is involved in supply chains where clear and obvious welfare benefits are provided to workers, their families and possibly the community. This may include healthcare, education and housing. An element of independent verification would normally be involved.

Grade B: The supplier makes regular visits to the factories and keeps B&Q fully informed regarding the sources of supply. The supplier has provided B&Q with sufficient evidence that the working conditions and health and safety are good (in comparison with the norm in that country).

Grade C: The supplier has an understanding of the issues and knows the sources of the products but has a limited awareness of the actual working conditions. Visits to the factories are too infrequent to enable the supplier to guarantee sound working conditions.

Grade D: The supplier demonstrates insufficient understanding of the supply chain for B&Q to be confident that there are no ethical concerns. Serious issues may have been identified and the supplier has not yet made a commitment to resolving them.

Grade E: There is a very poor understanding of the supply chain and sources of supply and the supplier shows no inclination to improve knowledge of the situation. Serious problems may have been identified, at the factory or elsewhere in the supply chain. These issues are unresolvable due to the scale of the problem or the attitude of the supplier or other key groups within the supply chain.

● B&Q's Toolkit

Appropriately for a DIY company, B&Q have developed an internal toolkit which is a 'portfolio of responses' for managing a particular supplier:

• Tool 1 is to terminate contracts with a particular supplier, an approach taken by B&Q in Pakistan when it decided that it could not be sure how bad child labour conditions were.

• Tool 2 is the certification option, whereby a product is certified as having been produced to internationally acceptable standards, e.g. Rugmark (see below).

- Tool 3, and B&Q's preferred option, is gradual improvement by working in close partnership with the factory management.
- Tool 4 is 'development through trade' where the emphasis is on bringing out long-standing and self-sustaining improvements in the community working with the people and players linked to the supply chain.

B&Q have published an evaluation of these tools (*B&Q: Being a Better Trading Neighbour*, September 1999).

● Assurance mechanisms
QUEST is currently an entirely internal and largely qualitative tool with no external third-party verification. Whilst this clearly gives room for weak implementation, the transparency with which B&Q report on the system has been commended by Christian Aid in their report Taking Stock which covers corporate performance on codes: *"If B&Q can do this and make the results public in an informative way, why do the main food retailers not do the same?"* The leadership and management intent of suppliers is an important element of B&Q's system. For example, when deciding whether or not to risk engaging with a sub-standard supplier, Knight says: *"There are only two key issues. Is the supply chain traceable? And are they prepared for a paradigm shift in how they work?... We decided a long time ago that the best way to protect ourselves is to fix the problems. Sweatshops are a business problem which business needs to solve."*

Collaborative initiatives, codes, certification – how useful?
B&Q have actively supported the Rugmark Foundation on the basis that it fits B&Q's values and makes good commercial sense. B&Q was the first UK retailer to sell Rugmark-certified rugs. Established by the Indo-German Export Promotion Council, this initiative certifies rugs to indicate to consumers that they are free from exploitative child labour. Children are allowed to work provided that this is within national legal limits and provided that they have access to education. The scheme makes unannounced visits to each loom at least every six months. Rugmark has set up several schools and also runs a Rehabilitation Centre for children who have been freed from exploitative conditions. Rugmark, according to B&Q's report, *Being a Better Trading Neighbour*, *"empowers [northern] retailers to state that illegal child labour is unacceptable in a way which prevents the need to impose a harmful boycott ... This has clearly caused a reaction in the industries and among politicians, catalysing action within India."*

As for other initiatives, B&Q is not keen to sign up to model codes, arguing that these are more about protecting corporate reputation than about cost effective ways of improving the condition in the supply chains. B&Q rejects the approach of making commitments to standards that it knows cannot be met. Knight argues that *"certification doesn't really work for cottage industries. We would only cover the last, and very minor, stage of the production. It wouldn't cover the really dangerous stages. A certificate just focuses the factory owner's attention on how to get the certificate and get round the difficult stuff."*

What will B&Q do if certification takes off? According to Knight, *"if the really big guys use the certificate as part of their marketing armoury, then we will have no choice but it won't add anything."* The real challenge for B&Q and other retailers lies in finding the right mechanisms to achieve and measure continuous improvement in working conditions as far down the supply chain as is realistic.

From principle to practice

The following case studies, referred to in Part I, Section 3, offer a range of examples of how three TNCs are approaching the challenges of implementing a human rights policy across corporate operations. Some are further advanced in this endeavour than others, but their starting point is the same – human rights cannot be avoided as a serious business issue.

BP Amoco – Exerting positive influence?

"Open markets, steady economic development and an open society are the conditions in which we can best pursue our business. This is contrary to the common belief that companies find it easier to deal with the apparent stability of repressive regimes than to manage the uncertainties of democracy. Stability built on repression is always false. Sooner or later the waters break the dam."

Sir John Browne, CEO, BP Amoco

BP Amoco's commitment to human rights

In early 1998, following extensive internal discussions, BP Amoco adopted a set of business policies describing the standard of care the company seeks to deliver. At the core of these policy commitments is the belief that the company's activities should generate economic benefits and opportunities and that their conduct should be a source of positive influence.

BP Amoco's Ethical Conduct Policy explicitly supports the principles set forth in the UN Universal Declaration on Human Rights and the ILO Tripartite Declaration of Principles concerning Multinational Enterprises and Social Policy. In addition its Relationships Policy commits the company to demonstrating respect for human dignity and the rights of individuals.

The policies are intended to provide a sound framework for conducting business in a manner that is supportive of human rights. Yet putting these

principles into practice presents many challenges. BP Amoco's responses to some of these challenges are considered below.

Strategic planning and human rights

It is much easier to avoid becoming embroiled in human rights controversies than to deal with the related practical and reputational risks. But can companies proactively plan to avoid the potential pitfalls? Before investing in new projects, BP Amoco now conducts a Country Risk Review. Amongst other factors, this process takes into consideration the social, political, cultural and human rights context of the country using a 20-year planning horizon. Market and shareholder risks are also important factors in the process, as are potential reputational risks.

The process involves a select number of internal staff from business units and the corporate centre, as well as external experts. The NGO Human Rights Watch has been invited to participate in a forthcoming Country

Risk Review, as human rights are of central concern to the country in question. One crucial question for BP Amoco to consider is whether it will be able to conduct a dialogue with the host Government. In some countries, BP Amoco's only contact with the Government is via the state-owned oil companies, which limits its capacity to pursue a policy of constructive engagement.

Rule of law

The Ethical Conduct Policy commits the company to respecting the rule of law in the countries of operation. But what about situations where national laws contravene basic human rights or where to uphold the letter of the law could result in human rights infringements? One such example is the apartheid laws of the old South Africa, which required racial segregation of the workforce. There, BP Amoco applied the principle that international law took precedence over national or local laws and chose to desegregate their employees. This policy extended to all aspects of its operations, salary scales and pension provisions, accommodation and leisure facilities.

BP Amoco respects the rule of law, recognising the hierarchy of international, regional, national and local laws. The company supports the establishment of the rule of law. Sound laws create greater investment certainty and reduce risk. By respecting the rule of law, BP Amoco is acknowledging that local or national laws may conflict with the promotion of human rights.

Partnership approaches to human rights

BP Amoco's enthusiasm for partnerships is directly applicable to the human rights arena. *"The notion that any corporation can make real progress on human rights issues without partnerships is naïve"* says David Rice, Director of BP Amoco's Policy Unit. The company's approach to partnerships is articulated in its Relationship Policy, which emphasises that long-term relationships, trust and mutual advantage are vital to business success.

The Relationship Policy guidelines are more explicit in committing the company, as part of its relations with governments, to work in partnership with others to resolve tensions or conflicts arising between international expectations on human rights and local or national practice. BP Amoco views this commitment as part of its mandate to make a constructive contribution to society. This is the motivation behind the company's ongoing support for the British-Angola Forum. Chaired by Human Rights Watch and based at the Royal Institute of International Affairs in London, the Forum aims to raise awareness about the development challenges and culture of Angola in an open forum. It brings together representatives from business, NGOs, government and the Angolan Embassy. BP Amoco's interest stems from the opportunity to improve its understanding of Angola, where BP

Amoco has offshore interests. It also views the Forum as having a potential role to play in conflict reduction and increased economic participation in Angola – both enormous challenges against the backdrop of continuing conflict between Government Forces and UNITA rebels.

The company distinguishes between different forms of partnership. It views dialogue with organisations such as Amnesty International and Human Rights Watch as invaluable in terms of the insights and political analysis it provides. At a more practical level, its latest efforts to support human rights and the development of human potential in Casanare, Colombia, is being developed through the World Bank's Business Partners for Development (BPD) initiative. This provides opportunities to benefit from the involvement and experiences of other natural resource development companies, NGOs and also the World Bank itself.

Advocacy versus influence

BP Amoco make a clear distinction between acting in an advocacy role for human rights and exerting a positive influence. *"Advocacy is rarely appropriate, as it can compromise our ability to exert a positive influence in the longer term"* says David Rice. This does not preclude BP Amoco from engaging in discussions with governments, for example, about the impact of unsustainable social or environmental policies on business. In practice, this must be managed in different ways in different situations-- sometimes publicly, sometimes quietly. Chris Gibson-Smith, one of BP Amoco's Managing Directors, recently gave a speech to the Communist Party School in Beijing, presenting BP Amoco's policies including support for the UDHR.

Where human rights abuses are of concern, BP Amoco's preference is to

stay rather than disinvest. *"The two main exceptions"* says David Rice *"are where our ability to maintain the safety and security of employees is compromised, and where it becomes impossible to operate in accordance with business policies"*. Clearly, the latter condition is open to interpretation, and in part depends on capacity to continue to exert a positive influence.

Moving outwards from the company's core operations where it has direct control, the company's 'ripples of influence' interact with many other influences at the global level, which, in turn, affects the company's ability to shape developments. This will vary between countries, issues and the prevailing social and political conditions. John Browne is convinced of the business case for exerting a positive influence. *"We don't believe in business standing up and lecturing governments"*, says Browne. *"What we do believe is that by engaging in the debate and by helping establish safe, stable and peaceful societies responsible business can promote good human rights behaviour. And where society thrives business thrives."*

Tools and training

BP Amoco's Ethical Conduct Policy is supported by more detailed policy explanations, to assist staff in resolving the dilemmas surrounding ethical decision-making. In addition, more detailed guidance on specific aspects of human rights is made available on the company's Intranet. This includes a decision-making model to help clarify issues and potential consequences, and advice on ethical issues such as bribery and corruption. The decision-making model is in essence a shared-judgement model — it poses a series of questions that helps staff identify when others should be involved in decision-making. BP Amoco's Intranet also includes links to the websites of the International Labour Organisation, the United Nations Human Rights Commissioner, Amnesty International and Human Rights Watch.

While some training has been given to staff in the form of workshops on ethical issues, the company is conscious of the need to equip staff more systematically to deal with human rights dilemmas. One innovative mechanism whereby experiences gained in one part of the company can be analysed and disseminated is through the peer review process. This process brings together centres of expertise on specific subjects within the group to review and challenge the performance of one of the business units.

Originally conceived as a technical review mechanism, the process has been applied to the company's dealings with indigenous peoples and to security provision. Following criticisms of BP Amoco's security agreement with the Colombian Army in Casanare, which the company accept was flawed, a new agreement was developed with advice from Human Rights Watch. The revised agreement, which is between Ecopetrol (BP Amoco's state-owned partner) and the Ministry of Defence, contains human rights and auditing provisions. Following a peer review process involving business units from Colombia and other countries where security is a major issue, best practice in security contracting arrangements are being adopted in other countries.

Assurance processes

BP Amoco's interpretation of policy assurance is that managers have the confidence to reassure the people they report to that policies are being implemented. This extends from line managers through to the Executive Vice President for Policies and Technology, who is ultimately responsible for assurance to the Group Chief Executive and the Board. In practical terms, assurance is generated by a number of activities and processes.

The annual certification process is one practical mechanism for providing assurance in the human rights arena on an annual basis. Each business unit leader must sign a letter indicating that all relevant staff have been made aware of the Ethical Conduct policy provisions, that they have an understanding of the human rights context of their operations, and that the operations are not resulting in human rights abuses. More proactively, they must also look for opportunities to promote human rights within the country of operation.

Measuring progress

Measuring progress on policy implementation is one of the challenges that BP Amoco is aiming to address. The company is supporting research into social indicators to help reinforce reporting on social performance, including human rights. This aspect is viewed as crucial by a number of NGOs if progress on

implementation of the Ethical Conduct policy is to stand up to objective evaluation. As Sofia Tickell of Oxfam observes: *"It is difficult to comment on the overall performance of BP Amoco with respect to human rights as the mechanisms for systematically capturing and reporting on progress are not in place"*. BP Amoco is equally convinced of the importance of finding the right mechanisms.

"A company which abuses its workforce or employs forced labour is not only in breach of the Universal Declaration of Human Rights, but is flying in the face of civilised thinking all over the world. And in a world of increasing transparency and global communication, such a company is also foolish if it thinks such behaviour will not attract attention. Even if moral imperatives are discarded, self-interest should dictate responsibility."

Peter Sutherland, Group Chairman, BP Amoco

Rio Tinto – Facing the challenge of implementation

"Human rights is a vast and complex subject. We need to understand better the boundaries between our responsibilities and those of the state in countries in which we operate."

Sir Robert Wilson, Chairman of Rio Tinto

By adopting an explicit policy commitment to human rights early in 1998, Rio Tinto has broken new ground in the human rights arena for the mining sector. With its policy framework established, the challenge now is to ensure consistent implementation of the policy throughout the group.

Defining the boundaries

Rio Tinto is conscious that the human rights continuum encompasses a broad spectrum of issues ranging from torture to employee rights through to the right to development. In defining the boundaries of its engagement on human rights issues Rio Tinto's primary focus has been on employees and human development. *"In this regard, there is clearly a disconnect between our focus and that of the wider public and the media, yet it is in these areas that we can make a tangible contribution,"* says Glynn Cochrane, Communities and Anthropology Advisor. This was the motivation behind Rio Tinto's Communities and Employees policies,[16] which complement its policy on human rights.

Policy commitment to human rights

Rio Tinto first published its human rights policy in early 1998 in the company's statement of Business Practice, *'The way we work'*. The motivation for explicitly articulating the values of the company was in part to help establish Rio Tinto as the 'developer of choice' – in line with its stated objective – and in part to respond to societies' increasing expectations of natural resource developers as corporate citizens.

The policy is based on Rio Tinto's *'support for the UN Universal Declaration of Human Rights and respect for the human rights provisions enshrined in the laws of those countries where the group operates'.*[17] It principally relates to the human rights of employees and communities, and clearly states that the Group has no mandate to act as a vehicle for global diplomacy nor to intervene beyond the immediate areas of influence of its operations. Operations are encouraged to promote broader understanding of human rights issues however, both in the interests of communities and in recognition that it is in Rio Tinto's strategic interest to be able to do business in stable and open societies.

The company's reluctance to engage in "global diplomacy" has been criticised by some NGOs, but Lord Holme, Advisor to the Chairman of Rio Tinto, makes a clear distinction between exerting positive influence and advocacy. *"Business is a greater power for good or ill than it sometimes wants to acknowledge, but the power of any one company acting alone to make a significant difference to the human condition is extremely limited".* Some NGOs, such as Amnesty International, would argue that these limitations do not apply within the sphere of a company's own operations, as Rio Tinto's policy explicitly accepts.

One area where Rio Tinto sees an opportunity to promote human rights at a more strategic level is through publicly supporting anti-corruption initiatives. The speech made by Chairman Sir Robert Wilson at the International Anti-corruption Conference organised by Transparency International in Durban in October 1999 is one such example.[18] Rio Tinto is also leading the Mining, Minerals and Sustainable Development project, an analytical study commissioned through the World Business Council for Sustainable Development by a group of 27 mining and mineral companies. Human rights are explicitly incorporated in the framework of the project.

Policies and assurance processes

The International Confederation of Free Trade Unions (ICFTU) has criticised the 'vague wording' of the policies in *'The way we work'*, which it claims conveys the impression that the statement is a public relations exercise. While Rio Tinto strongly rejects this assertion, the company is keen to improve assurance processes for the policy commitments in 'The way we work'. Specifically in the human rights arena, an internal primer is being prepared to demonstrate the relevance of human rights to the operations. The primer will also illustrate practical approaches to dealing with human rights issues for operational staff.

Security is one of the aspects that will be addressed in the primer. As background, a group-wide survey on security has been undertaken to determine risks to the operations, the origins of risks (such as disenfranchised minorities) and current security

16. The Communities Policy was introduced in 1997
17. The Way We Work: Our statement of business practice. Rio Tinto, 1998.
18. See Rio Tinto's website www.riotinto.com

arrangements. This will help to define more accurately the target audience within the group for additional guidance, as well as capturing current practices.

What also needs to be addressed, according to Amnesty International, is the risk that the communities affected by Rio Tinto's activities may have their human rights violated by security forces if they engage in non-violent protest against aspects of the company's operations which adversely affect them.

Finally, an internal review of assurance mechanisms is also in progress that is starting to identify areas for improvement and possible approaches. Options under consideration include external verification of community engagement and a system of internal assurance letters devoted to the company's social policies. This would draw upon the experience of companies such as Shell and BP Amoco.

Human development and human rights

Helping to meet human development aspirations is at the heart of the Communities Policy, with its focus on community development planning. The policy was developed through an extensive internal consultative process and supported by regional conferences to explain the intent. The company requires all operations to submit *'Five-Year Plans'* based on an appraisal of baseline socio-economic conditions and consultation with communities. The plans identify socio-economic and capacity building programmes that are developed in partnership with communities and set performance targets over five years. For developing country operations in particular, this presents an opportunity to enhance social infrastructure in a planned manner.

The model of developing socio-economic programmes in parallel with

the project planning process is rapidly gaining ground within the mining sector, but Rio Tinto has broken new ground in applying the same principles systematically to all group operations irrespective of their stage of development. In Madagascar for example, a baseline socio-economic assessment for the QIT Madagascar Minerals proposed minerals sands project highlighted the inter-linkages between poverty and environmental degradation. It also identified the risks to sustainable resources management and economic development (and therefore to Rio Tinto) of proceeding with the project in isolation from a broader development strategy. This led the company to develop partnerships with government and donor agencies to establish a regional development strategy to maximise synergies from the project.

The Kelian gold mine in East Kalimantan, Indonesia, has been operational since 1992 and will cease operation in 2003. It has attracted the attention of NGOs, in particular Community Aid Abroad in Australia, who have raised concerns on behalf of the local indigenous peoples over inadequate compensation for loss of land, access to resources and environmental damages. Artisanal small-scale mining, despite the inherent safety risks (e.g. in 1999 eight artisanal miners lost their lives) was a source of income for local communities. This practice was declared illegal, with the advent of formal mining, resulting in police harassment of those who continued. The five-year closure planning process at Kelian highlighted these and other issues. Rio Tinto and Kelian Equitorial Mining have been in discussion with communities surrounding the mine concerning grievances against their operations. These negotiations, which began in 1998, have been facilitated by WALHI (the Indonesian affiliate of Friends of the Earth) and a number of East Kalimantan NGOs. Kelian is one of

the Focus Projects for the World Bank's Business Partners for Development (BPD) initiative, through which Rio Tinto's aim is to apply best practices to the closure of the mine.

More generally, work is currently in progress to develop indicators to measure progress on implementation of Five-Year Plans. These in turn will assist in providing locally relevant information for site-based reporting to communities, which Rio Tinto has committed to introducing throughout the group. The option of having an external review of the developing relationship between operations and communities is also envisaged. This would involve third parties, perhaps a local NGO, in assisting all parties to select priorities for future action.

Opposing infringements of human rights

As well as referring to the company's support for the Universal Declaration, Rio Tinto's Human Rights Policy specifically requires the operations to oppose infringements of the rights of employees and local communities. Operations encountering such cases are required to draw up a strategy for dealing with them, either through private dialogue, public action, or a combination of both.

Rio Tinto sees the protection of human rights in this context as a logical extension of its policy commitments to employees and to communities, which emphasise contributing to their development through a relationship based on mutual respect. As Robert Court, Rio Tinto's Corporate Relations Manager and Co-ordinator on Sustainable Development Issues observes, *"how can we meaningfully contribute to the development of human potential if basic rights are being infringed?"*

While human rights are of concern in a number of countries where Rio Tinto operates, the Freeport-McMoRan Grasberg mine[19] in the Indonesian province of Irian Jaya has attracted a lot of negative attention from both environmental and human rights NGOs. The NGO concerns centre on human rights abuses of indigenous people throughout Irian Jaya and in the vicinity of the mine, in part resulting from loss and damage to ancestral lands and in part linked to the Indonesian military's suppression of the Free Papua Movement (OPM). The social landscape today is complicated by Indonesia's failure to allow a representative ballot on independence in 1969, its subsequent transmigration of over 200,000 Indonesians to Irian Jaya under the repressive administration of Suharto, and by Freeport's failure to account for indigenous perspectives on land ownership in the early days of the project in the late 1960s. The company refutes this by pointing to the 'January Agreement' of 1974, *"the first agreement in all of Indonesia to recognise the land rights of indigenous peoples"*.

One of the challenges Rio Tinto and other major resource development companies often face as a result of joint-venture arrangements or acquisitions is how to reconcile differing corporate cultures. In 1999 Freeport adopted a Social and Human Rights Policy that emphasises the need to build relationships with indigenous communities based on an improved cultural understanding. It also explicitly commits the company to promote and protect human rights. Following this policy commitment, the company points to its decision in early 2000 to provide human rights training for all employees, an annual certification process, and the appointment of a senior judge as special counsel on human rights to the Freeport Chairman and CEO. The challenge of implementing this policy lies in extending it to all parts of the company's operations.

Employee rights, association and representation

Rio Tinto's Employees Policy prohibits discrimination on any grounds. The only possible exception is where it is *"apparent that a particular effort should be made to employ people from local communities"*. One such exception is on the remote Island of Lihir in Papua New Guinea (PNG) where 4% of Lihir Gold's 2000-strong workforce is drawn from the Island's population of 8250. A further 45% are employed from elsewhere in PNG.

Rio Tinto's employment practices on Lihir created tensions between PNG nationals and local communities, which highlights the difficulties of achieving an equitable balance. The use of non-Lihirian PNG labour ensured that some employment benefits accrued to the country, but caused discontent amongst local communities. Conversely, excessive reliance on local workers would have generated more goodwill, but exacerbated post-construction social impacts. Disparities in the number of employees drawn from local villages gave rise to complaints that villages in the immediate vicinity of the mine were favoured for project employment. However, the challenge for Rio Tinto was to balance the need to compensate those most adversely impacted with providing benefits equitably to all communities.

One other locally 'controversial' aspect of Rio Tinto's employment practices on Lihir stems from the fact that 25% of Lihirian employees are women.[20] Although Lihirian society is matrilineal, in practice the subservience of women is institutionalised in traditional clan structures and in their traditional roles of gardening, household tasks and child rearing. The company's attempts to promote non-discriminatory employment practices while respecting customary norms, illustrates some of the complexities of adhering to universal employment rights principles.

Employment practices in some of Rio Tinto's Australian operations have been heavily criticised by local trade unions and the International Federation of Chemical, Energy, Mines and General Workers' Unions (ICEM), which published 'Rio Tinto: Behind the Façade'. In particular, this document alleges that the company is anti-union and refuses to recognise unions for bargaining purposes in contravention of two core ILO conventions (No.87 and No.98).

In response, Rio Tinto claims that it respects the right of employees to belong to a trade union, or not, which has created tensions in some Australian operations. It also claims to support collective representation, either through a union or any other medium that employees may choose. Andrew Vickerman, Rio Tinto's Head of External Affairs, emphasises the need to make a distinction between employment practices that are exploitative or abusive and clearly in breach of human rights, as opposed to those where perceptions differ depending on philosophy. For example, this might include hiring and retrenching on merit as opposed to hiring only from union lists or retrenching solely on years of service.

Conclusion

Increasingly, companies are starting to recognise the relevance of human rights to their activities and their potential to have a positive or negative influence on such rights. In articulating its policy commitment to human rights, Rio Tinto has begun to engage with some of the concerns that trade unions and NGOs have been raising regarding the human rights context of its operations. It has also expressed a willingness to oppose infringements of these rights. In the prevailing 'show me' rather than 'tell me' culture, the challenge for Rio Tinto and others lies in finding the right mechanisms to provide assurances that the policy is being systematically put into practice.

Rio Tinto – Facing the challenge of implementation

---

19. Rio Tinto has a 13% stake in Grasberg and 40% in an expansion project.
20. The company employment statistics cited in this paper date from mid-1998.

Levi Strauss – Forming multi-stakeholder partnerships

Levi Strauss & Co., a privately-owned US company, is the world's largest brand-name apparel manufacturer with sales in 1998 of $6 billion. The company owns brands including Levi's, Dockers and Slates and employs 30,000 people world-wide. It has a head start on many human and labour rights issues given that it was the first transnational company in its sector to adopt a code. But perhaps most importantly, it has consistently used a multi-stakeholder approach to develop and implement its policy on working conditions. This case study focuses on an ambitious pilot project to test civil society involvement in third party verification in the Dominican Republic.

First off the block

In 1991, a cross-departmental project team began a two-year project that involved 25 internal and external stakeholder groups. It also conducted research on the conditions that workers experienced in the 600-700 sub-contracting units which are based in 50-60 countries. The team considered the various needs and concerns of all parties. This process led to the formulation and adoption of guidelines, Levi Strauss's "Terms of Engagement" (ToE), in 1992. In-country managers became responsible for ensuring the implementation of these ToEs and were given specialist auditor training to do so.

Finding a credible civil society verification process

Over the last seven years, Levi Strauss has been testing more intensive forms of multi-stakeholder engagement. This is part of the evolution of an internal monitoring process that has gone from a simple Q&A session to a detailed review about the do's and don'ts of implementing the key human rights elements. This has been an evolving process, the most recent step being a pilot project in the Dominican Republic (DR) which was designed to help answer the question of how to make internal monitoring more effective and therefore credible.

The problem is this. Professional auditors can be too expensive, can fail to understand the local situation well enough, can have insufficient access to workers to be able properly to verify the most important human rights issues, and can have limited credibility for the social verification task. Unions are perhaps the obvious 'social partner' for this sort of work but the business-union relationship is often very tense, with mutual recriminations and an adversarial history. Labour-friendly NGOs who have the credibility to verify working conditions are often not well equipped for the task. And those NGOs who have the best capacity and credibility for this role often have the least developed relationship with contractors. Given this situation, Miriam Rodriguez, Levi Strauss's Latin America Regional Manager saw only one way forward: *"We believed that if you could bring everyone to the table, we could achieve a better solution than any one party could do alone."*

Build contractor support and ownership at the outset

The Levi Strauss in-country managers met with their DR contractors to determine whether an innovative partnership could be developed between the company, its contractors and NGOs. All four contractors – D'Clase Corp., Grupo M, Interamericana and RK Fashion – gave the project a green light.

Choose your NGO partners carefully

Levi Strauss then asked an intermediary organisation, US-based Business for Social Responsibility, to help identify potential NGO partners. Having a credible and informed third party was very important in helping Levi Strauss find the right partners, and in convincing NGOs that they were not being engaged for company PR purposes.

The criteria for selecting the NGOs were demanding. The NGOs needed to:
- have an understanding of workplace standards and local laws;
- be focused on improving peoples living and working conditions and on social progress;
- be well-respected in the community and by other NGOs;
- be able to maintain impartiality and objectivity.

The NGOs selected were the national office of OXFAM (an international development NGO), Latin American Faculty of Social Sciences (a federation of research groups), Programme for Community Intervention (with a well-developed methodology of participatory research) and Research Centre for Feminist Action (with a focus on women's issues).

It was a delicate balancing act to bring the different parties together and there was a degree of mutual mistrust at the outset. Levi Strauss gave the NGOs a free hand in visiting production facilities and talking to workers. Vice President of Grupo M, one of the contractors, Joseph Blumberg acknowledged *"the nice thing was that* the NGOs were the first to acknowledge that they were surprised. We also appreciated that they didn't just focus on 'are you allowed to unionise?' but also asked about the full range of things – health, safety, welfare..."

Given the low starting levels of trust, what allowed the contractors to allow independent NGOs to wander around generally unsupervised? Rodriguez identifies the crucial importance of agreeing on the scope, expectations, resource, timing and above all, the methodology of the research process. The NGOs developed the research methodology, experienced the training that Levi Strauss managers get first-hand, reviewed the ToE materials, conducted the site visits and interviews, and prepared their report.

Start from the common ground and work outwards

The Levi Strauss team involved in the project included representatives from Global Operations, US Operations and Sourcing, Dominican Republic office, Government Affairs, Community Affairs, Communications and Human Resources. The company's team was culturally diverse which was an important factor in breaking down some of the NGOs' stereotypes of a US company, and helped to build trust. While the relationships developed in an open and non-adversarial manner for the most part, there were inevitable rough patches in the process. According to Rodriguez: *"You have very different organisational cultures here. Business thinks timelines and quick fixes. One of the things businesses had to learn was that there are some things that just cannot be rushed. NGOs tend to be more cerebral and look for the optimal solution."* The key to overall success was a set of shared objectives and a clearly defined process agreed by all parties from the outset. Levi Strauss points to two important achievements from this collaboration;

• Confidence about the current audit process and agreement on key improvements: all the participants feel the project has succeeded at several levels. Most practically, it has identified where the internal auditing process is working and where it is not (e.g. the need for more worker involvement in the monitoring of the codes). Levi Strauss and the contractors have accepted all the recommendations.

• An ongoing contractor-NGO relationship: the project has resulted in the NGOs and contractors deciding to work together on an ongoing basis. According to Rodriguez: *"There has been continued post-event dialogue and there's mutual respect. Both recognise they have a joint problem with health care. They both want to get wider change in the sector – other contractors need to come on board. Contractors have a heightened awareness of the issues and see the business benefits."*

The Director of the Research Centre for Feminist Action (CIPAF), Magaly Pineda, confirms this assessment. She highlights the difference between how women are treated by Levi Strauss contractors and by the average contractor: *"If you are a woman, before you can get a job with many of the non-Levi Strauss contractors, the first thing you have to do is get a pregnancy test to show you are not pregnant. But with Levi Strauss contractors, it is so different – they even have a pregnancy club!"* The Managing Director of Grupo M, Fernando Capellan is also President of the DR Association of Industrial Free Zones and in this capacity paid for and sent out 600 copies of the CIPAF's Spanish language booklet for workers about codes to all the factories.

No short cuts
There is little doubt that Levi Strauss contractors are amongst the most

responsible employers in the Dominican Republic. But how much of the present situation is related to Levi Strauss' monitoring process and how much is related to their initial choice of good practice suppliers? Grupo M, for example, has a long-standing record of making the *"most progressive advancements of the past 20 years within this sector"*, according to US Council for Economic Priorities which gave the company its "Employee Empowerment Award" in 1998. Initial selection and on-going standards' monitoring are important components, alongside other factors such as purchasing price, but perhaps the most important thing is the underlying ethos of long-term partnerships (see box on Grupo M).

Corporate culture is key
Many companies would delay having outsiders, especially NGOs who cannot be controlled through contractual relationships, come into the process until they are sure things are sufficiently acceptable. Rodriguez believes it is often in involving 'outsiders' that the question of what is acceptable is answered. So could Levi Strauss and the contractors have undertaken this third party process earlier, given that it adopted the Terms of Engagement in 1992? Perhaps, but it takes time to develop a supportive culture within the company for taking these kinds of risks, as well as to persuade business partners to participate. The personal commitment and leadership of CEO Bob Haas, who continually asks *"is this the best we can do?"*, has been at the heart of developing a corporate culture which strives for continuous improvement.

Levi Strauss – Forming multi-stakeholder partnerships

Grupo M

Grupo M, a privately-owned company, is the oldest Levi Strauss contractor in the Dominican Republic. In a frank assessment of its performance before it signed up to Levi Strauss's Terms of Engagement, Joseph Blumberg, Grupo M's Vice President says *"We did not mistreat our workers in any way but in comparison to now, what we did was very basic."* Acknowledging that at the start, their motivation was *"to do what an important customer wanted"*, Blumberg also highlights an important and unforeseen development: *"Over time we began to realise that there were very real benefits – workers respond so well to this kind of approach. So we have now gone well beyond Levi Strauss requirements."*

What has motivated this development? Grupo M have found significant bottom-line benefits including: very low absenteeism; low staff turnaround after vacation; no strikes. This allows Grupo M to meet quality standards that have allowed it to win contracts from all the major brands as customers (including M&S, Liz Claiborne, Polo, etc). In addition to these straight business issues Blumberg also highlights another motive: *"Our workers come from a sector of society that faces big social problems. A responsible company can't just shut off to that."*

The process of becoming a responsible employer has involved significant financial investment in terms of worker benefits. But according to Blumberg, *"the biggest thing has been the mindset change. It had to start with top management otherwise it would have been no use. Before, I would not really have cared about eye shields and needle guards so long as my production figures were OK."* So what kind of things does Grupo M now do? It subsidises transportation, runs day care centres, has an extensive medical and dental service for its workers and their families, provides training at many levels (e.g. literacy right through to higher qualifications so that former operators can become factory managers). Blumberg is unequivocal when asked whether this is something which only very special companies should do. *"No! Everyone will get benefit just from meeting the basic code. We have chosen to go further and get extra benefit for being seen as leaders and trend-setters."*

On the difficult question of unions, Blumberg says: *"We accept the right to associate, but our workers haven't gone for unions. The better you treat people, the more you give back to them, the more you recognise that you are where you are because of what they are doing, the more harmony there will be in your relationship. And then why do you need a union? A union is there to help workers get along with management."*

This view is not shared by Neil Kearney, General Secretary of the International Textile, Garment and Leather Workers Federation who sees workplace issues as complex affairs, and considers that untrained monitors can often be deceived by appearances. Says Kearney: *"Some factories are clean and offer reasonably good working conditions, yet workers are denied the right to organise…Monitoring is not something to be carried out by trade unions or NGOs. Trade unions should be monitoring workplaces in the interests of their members, not in the interests of a code of conduct, which is essentially a management tool. As for NGOs, their role as campaigners for improved working conditions is often greatly compromised when they try to carry out continuous monitoring. Theirs should be more of a watchdog role. Verification should be carried out by professionals trained in factory inspection skills and working to clearly defined and documented monitoring methods."*

The process which Grupo M have started looks set to continue. According to Blumberg, developing country contractors have no alternative but to adapt: *"It's just the way of the world. This is about a change in worldwide consciousness. You can't keep getting work from people when you are not willing to treat them fairly. The train is moving – in some countries slowly maybe and in other countries faster – but it is moving. And businesses can either get on board or get off."*

3 Resources

Resources

Guidelines for good practice

Human rights from the perspective of business and industry:
a checklist compiled by the Norwegian Confederation of Business and Industry

This checklist is a tool for companies devising their own strategies for dealing with human rights in accordance with internationally recognised human rights standards within their own operations. It takes as its framework the UN Universal Declaration of Human Rights (UDHR) drawn up in 1948. The Declaration refers to fundamental values which every system of justice must respect and protect out of consideration for the individual. All UN member states have ratified the UDHR. The document has achieved common law status and its principles have been incorporated into the constitutions of many nations.

Although not exhaustive, the checklist offers a reference point for corporate managers who wish to ensure that their company pursues a policy that complies with international human rights standards. In some cases, the areas addressed will be covered by national legislation. Where such national legislation maintains a higher standard than international legislation for the protection of human rights, companies should follow the national laws. Where, on the other hand, national legislation does not take sufficient account of human rights, companies should take international human rights standards as the basis for their policies in the relevant area.

Those articles in the UDHR most relevant to companies have been selected, followed by questions which companies should address as they seek to formulate policies which adhere to international human rights standards. Occasional references are also made to key ILO conventions of relevance to the checklist.

Right to freedom from discrimination

The UDHR, Article 2: "Everyone is entitled to all the rights and freedoms set forth in this Declaration, without distinction of any kind, such as race, colour, sex, language, religion, political or other opinion, national or social origin, property, birth or other status."

- Does the company have guidelines that prohibit discrimination based on race, colour, sex, language, religion, political or other opinion, national or social origin, property, birth or other status – and are these guidelines enforced in connection with recruitment, training and promotions?
- Has the company drawn up guidelines that comply with ILO Convention No. 111 (1958), which prohibits sexual discrimination?
- Does the company have guidelines to ensure that its products and services are accessible to every potential customer, without prejudice on the grounds of personal characteristics or identity?
- Does the company have guidelines to prevent sexual harassment at work?
- Does the company make efforts to determine whether potential business associates, suppliers and partners have any explicit policy in the above-mentioned areas?

The right to personal safety and security

The UDHR, Article 3: "Everyone has the right to life, liberty and security of person."

- Does the company have guidelines which ensure safe and healthy working conditions for employees, and are the rules observed?
- Where the company uses private security guards, have guidelines been drawn up to determine acceptable actions/courses of action that can be implemented against people who

represent a threat to the company's security?
- Where the company uses public police or security guards, have guidelines been drawn up to determine exactly when and how they should be used, especially in situations in which one has experienced that the same personnel have represented a threat to the local populace?
- Where the company makes goods or services that can potentially be used to violate human rights or for end products that can be used for such violations, have control procedures been instituted to keep the products from falling into the wrong hands?
- If management were to learn that the company's products or services had been used to violate people's life, liberty or personal security, does it have rules that can be applied to prevent further business contact with such trading partners?

Ban on slavery

The UDHR, Article 4: "No one shall be held in slavery or servitude; slavery and the slave trade shall be prohibited in all their forms."

- Does the company have procedures that prevent slavery, forced child labour or hard labour performed by prisoners?
- Does the company have guidelines that prevent collaboration, trade and partnership with or deliveries from enterprises that use slaves, forced child labour or hard labour performed by prisoners?
- Does the company fulfil the standards set out in the UN Convention on the Rights of the Child and ILO Conventions No. 29 (1930) concerning Forced Labour and No. 138 (1973) concerning Minimum Age?

Ban on torture

The UDHR, Article 5: "No one shall be subjected to torture or to cruel, inhuman or degrading treatment or punishment."

- Does the company have procedures in place to prevent it from dealing with business associates that employ corporal punishment or other forms of physical or mental pressure on their employees?
- If the company uses private-sector security guards, has it (or the security company being used) drawn up rules to ensure that the security personnel do not employ methods that might be construed as torture or cruel, inhuman, or degrading treatment or punishment?
- Have the security guards received training in compliance with the UN Code of Conduct for Law Enforcement Personnel?

The right to freedom of opinion and expression

The UDHR, Article 19: "Everyone has the right to freedom of opinion and expression; this right includes freedom to hold opinions without interference and to seek, receive and impart information and ideas through any media and regardless of frontiers."

- Has the company prepared guidelines that recognise and protect employees' right to freedom of opinion and expression?
- Does the company make efforts to determine whether potential business associates, sub-contractors and partners have an explicit policy in this area?

The right to freedom of peaceful assembly and association

The UDHR, Article 20: "1) Everyone has the right to freedom of peaceful assembly and association. 2) No one may be compelled to belong to an association."

- Has the company considered, or possibly prepared procedures to prevent the authorities from intervening in employees' right to freedom of peaceful assembly and association? How would the company respond if an order were issued to dissolve the trade unions, and threats were made to imprison company employees?
- Has the company drawn up guidelines that forbid it from intervening in employees' freedom of association and their right to organise, for example, through threats of termination on the grounds of trade union activism?
- Has the company familiarised its employees with the international ILO regulations concerning the protection of the right of assembly and association, particularly ILO Conventions No. 87 (1948) and No. 98 (1949)?
- Does the company make efforts to determine whether potential business associates, sub-contractors and partners have a comparable policy in respect of these rights?

The right to free participation in political life

The UDHR, Article 21: "1) Everyone has the right to take part in the government of his/her country, directly or through freely chosen representatives. 2) Everyone has the right to equal access to public service in his/her country. 3) The will of the people shall be the basis of the authority of government; this will shall be expressed in periodic and genuine elections which shall be by universal and equal suffrage and shall be held by secret vote or by equivalent free voting procedures."

- Has the company drawn up guidelines that prohibit intervention into or a reduction of employees' right to participate freely in their country's government or to equal access to public service in their country?
- Does the corporation/company make efforts to determine whether business associates, partners or sub-contractors have guidelines in this area?

The right to work

The UDHR, Article 23: "1) Everyone has the right to work, to free choice of employment, to just and favourable conditions of work and to protection against unemployment. 2) Everyone, without any discrimination, has the right to equal pay for equal work. 3) Everyone who works has the right to just and favourable remuneration, ensuring for him/herself and his/her family an existence worthy of human dignity, and supplemented, if necessary, by other means of social protection. 4) Everyone has the right to form and to join trade unions for the protection of his/her interests."

- Has the company drawn up guidelines that help ensure the right of employees and future employees to free choice of employment, to just and favourable conditions of work, and to protection against arbitrary or unjust unemployment?
- Has the company drawn up guidelines to prevent discrimination in connection with hiring on the grounds of ethnic background, nationality, philosophy of life, religion, cultural characteristics or political views?
- Does the company have guidelines that guarantee equal pay for equal work?
- Does the company have guidelines that prohibit intervention in employees' right to freely form or join trade unions to protect their interests?
- Does the company have guidelines that ensure employees' right to enter into collective agreements, including their right to strike?
- Is it important to the company that partners and suppliers do not have discriminatory hiring practices and that they do what they can to ensure a safe, healthy environment for their employees?

The right to rest and leisure

The UDHR, Article 24: "Everyone has the right to rest and leisure, including reasonable limitation of working hours and periodic holidays with pay."

- Has the company drawn up guidelines that ensure employees' right to rest and leisure?
- Does the company have regular working hours that ensure employees a reasonable limit on their working hours?
- Does the company make efforts to determine whether potential business associates, partners, and suppliers have similar guidelines in this area?

The right to an adequate standard of living

The UDHR, Article 25: "1) Everyone has the right to a standard of living adequate for the health and well-being of him/herself and of his/her family, including food, clothing, housing and medical care and necessary social services, and the right to security in the event of unemployment, sickness, disability, widowhood, old age or other lack of livelihood in circumstances beyond his/her control. 2) Motherhood and childhood are entitled to special care and assistance. All children, whether born in or out of wedlock, shall enjoy the same social protection."

- Has the company devised guidelines and schemes to help ensure the survival of employees who have had to resign due to circumstances beyond their control? The phrase 'such schemes' refers, e.g., to pension schemes, health and retirement insurance, rental housing, emergency contingency schemes, etc.
- Has the company drawn up guidelines and schemes that permit absence due to the illness of children without this having any effect on the employment situation?
- Does the company make efforts to determine whether business associates, partners and suppliers

have developed similar arrangements for their employees?

The right to education

The UDHR, Article 26: " Everyone has the right to education. Education shall be free, at least in the elementary and fundamental stages. Elementary education shall be compulsory. Technical and professional education shall be made generally available and higher education shall be equally accessible to all on the basis of merit."

- Has the company drawn up guidelines to prevent child labour when such labour means eliminating or reducing children's right to education?
- Has the company devised training and human resources development programmes to enable employees to improve their skills and qualifications?
- Does the company make efforts to determine whether potential business associates, partners or suppliers follow similar guidelines?

The right of minorities and indigenous peoples to protect their identity

The UN Convention on Civil and Political Rights, Article 27:
"In those States in which ethnic, religious or linguistic minorities exist, persons belonging to such minorities shall not be denied the right, in community with the other members of their group, to enjoy their own culture, to profess and practise their own religion, or to use their own language."

- Does the company recognise the right of minorities and indigenous peoples to protect and respect their cultural identity and integrity?
- Does it acknowledge the moral and material interests collateral to this right?
- Has the company drawn up guidelines that specifically ensure employees who belong to minorities the right to practice their own

culture, profess and practice their own religion, and use their own language?

- Has the company familiarised its employees with the international ILO regulations on the protection of indigenous peoples, particularly ILO Convention No. 169 (1989)?
- Does the company recognise that employees who belong to minorities or indigenous populations must not be subject to discrimination because they belong to a minority or have indigenous origins?
- Does the company attach importance to whether potential business associates, partners and suppliers follow the same guidelines?

Other important international human rights instruments

Global conventions

The International Covenant on Civil and Political Rights, 1966
The International Covenant on Economic, Social and Cultural Rights, 1966
The UN Convention against Racial Discrimination, 1965
The UN Convention against Sexual Discrimination, 1979
The UN Convention against Torture, 1984
The UN Children's Convention, 1989

Regional conventions

The Council of Europe's Human Rights Convention, 1950, with optional protocols
The Council of Europe's Torture Convention, 1987
The American Human Rights Convention, 1978
The African Charter on Human and People's Rights, 1984

ILO conventions/declarations

ILO Convention No. 29 concerning Forced Labour
ILO Convention No. 87 concerning Freedom of Association and Protection of the Right to Organize
ILO Convention No. 98 concerning the Right to Organize and Collective Bargaining
ILO Convention No. 105 concerning the Abolition of Forced Labour
ILO Convention No. 111 concerning Discrimination (Employment and Occupation)
ILO Convention No. 138 concerning Minimum Age
ILO Convention No. 169 concerning Indigenous and Tribal Peoples in Autonomous States
ILO Declaration (1998) concerning Fundamental Human Rights at Work.

This checklist is reproduced by kind permission of NHO, the Norwegian Confederation of Business and Industry. www.nho.no

1. **Company policy on human rights.** All companies should adopt an explicit company policy on human rights which includes public support for the Universal Declaration of Human Rights. Companies should establish procedures to ensure that all operations are examined for their potential impact on human rights, and safeguards to ensure that company staff are never complicit in human rights abuses. The company policy should enable discussion with the authorities at local, provincial and national levels of specific cases of human rights violations and the need for safeguards to protect human rights. It should enable the establishment of programs for the effective human rights education and training of all employees within the company and encourage collective action in business associations to promote respect for international human rights standards.

2. **Security.** All companies should ensure that any security arrangements protect human rights and are consistent with international standards for law enforcement. Any security personnel employed or contracted should be adequately trained. Procedures should be consistent with the United Nations (UN) Basic Principles on the Use of Force and Firearms by Law Enforcement Officials and the UN Code of Conduct for Law Enforcement Officials. They should include measures to prevent excessive force, as well as torture or cruel, inhuman or degrading treatment. Companies should develop clear rules for calling in or contracting with state security forces and for not hiring security personnel who have been responsible for serious human rights violations. Any complaint about security procedures or personnel should be promptly and independently investigated. Companies which supply military, security or police products or services should take stringent steps to prevent those products and services from being misused to commit human rights violations.

3. **Community engagement.** All companies should take reasonable steps to ensure that their operations do not have a negative impact on the enjoyment of human rights by the communities in which they operate. This should include a willingness to meet with community leaders and voluntary organizations to discuss the role of the company within the broader community. Companies should seek to support activities and organizations which promote human rights, for example by supporting education, training or citizenship programs which incorporate human rights issues and organizations which defend human rights.

4. **Freedom from discrimination.** All companies should ensure that their policies and practices prevent discrimination based on ethnic origin, sex, colour, language, national or social origin, economic status, religion, political or other conscientiously held beliefs, birth or other status. This should include recruitment, promotion, remuneration, working conditions, customer relations and the practices of contractors, suppliers and partners. It should include measures to deal with sexual or racial harassment, and to prohibit national, racial or religious hatred.

5. **Freedom from slavery.** All companies should ensure that their policies and practices prohibit the use of chattel slaves, forced labour, bonded child labourers or coerced prison labour. This should include ensuring that suppliers, partners or contractors do not use such labour.

6. **Health and safety.** All companies should ensure that their policies and practices provide for safe and healthy working conditions and products. The company should not engage in or support the use of corporal punishment, mental or physical coercion, or verbal abuse.

7. **Freedom of association and the right to collective bargaining.** All companies should ensure that all employees are able to exercise their rights to freedom of expression, peaceful assembly and association, as well as a fair means of collective bargaining without discrimination, including the right to form trade unions and to strike. Companies have a responsibility to ensure such rights for their employees even if such rights are not protected in a particular country's national law. Companies should take steps to ensure that suppliers, partners or contractors do not infringe such rights.

8. **Fair working conditions.** All companies should ensure just and favourable conditions of work, reasonable job security and fair and adequate remuneration and benefits. This should include provision for an adequate standard of living for employees and their families. Companies should take steps to ensure that suppliers, partners or contractors do not infringe such rights.

9. **Monitoring human rights.** All companies should establish mechanisms to monitor effectively all their operations' compliance with codes of conduct and international human rights standards. Such mechanisms must be credible and all reports must periodically be independently verifiable in a similar way to the auditing of accounts or

1. Published in 1998

the quality of products and services. Other stakeholders such as members of local communities in which the company operates and voluntary organizations should have an opportunity to contribute in order to ensure transparency and credibility.

Sources in International Human Rights Standards
The following are the international human rights standards upon which these principles are based. They are taken from: the Universal Declaration of Human Rights (UDHR), Conventions of the International Labour Organisation (ILO), the United Nations (UN) Basic Principles on the Use of Force and Firearms, the UN Code of Conduct for Law Enforcement Officials and the ILO Tripartite Declaration of Principles Concerning Multinational Enterprises and Social Policy.

Other international human rights standards are also essential sources for the development of respect for human rights by companies. Treaties which should be promoted include the International Covenant on Civil and Political Rights, the International Covenant on Economic, Cultural and Social Rights, the Convention Against Torture and Other Cruel, Inhuman or Degrading Treatment or Punishment, the Convention on the Elimination of All Forms of Discrimination against Women, the Convention on the Rights of the Child, the International Convention on the Elimination of All Forms of Racial Discrimination, and the International Convention on the Rights of All Migrant Workers and Members of Their Families.

Further relevant international standards may include the Organization for Economic Cooperation and Development Guidelines for Multinational Enterprises, and the Principles Governing Conventional Arms Transfers of the Organization for Security Cooperation in Europe, even though such standards are not international law.

1. Company Policy on Human Rights
Universal Declaration of Human Rights, preamble: *The UDHR is proclaimed as a common standard of achievement for all peoples and all nations: "to the end that every individual and every organ of society, keeping this Declaration constantly in mind, shall strive by teaching and education to promote respect for these rights and freedoms and by progressive measures, national and international, to secure their universal and effective recognition and observance, both among the peoples of member States themselves and among the peoples of territories under their jurisdiction"*

The OECD Guidelines for Multinational Enterprises state that: *"Every state has the right to prescribe the conditions under which multinational enterprises operate within its national jurisdiction subject to international law and to the international agreements to which it has subscribed..."*

2. Security
UDHR Article 3: *"Everyone has the right to life, liberty and security of person"*

UDHR Article 5: *"No one shall be subjected to torture or to cruel, inhuman or degrading treatment or punishment."*

UDHR Article 9: *"No one shall be subjected to arbitrary arrest, detention or exile"*

UN Code of Conduct for Law Enforcement Officials includes provisions that: *"...(2) In the performance of their duty, law enforcement officials shall respect and protect human dignity and maintain and uphold the human rights of all persons. (3) Law enforcement officials may use force only when strictly necessary and to the extent required for the performance of their duty." (4) matters of a confidential nature in the possession of law enforcement officials shall be kept confidential, unless the performance of duty or the needs of justice strictly require otherwise (5) No law enforcement official may inflict, instigate or tolerate any act of torture or other cruel, inhuman, degrading treatment or punishment, nor may a law enforcement official invoke superior orders or exceptional circumstances such as a state of war or a threat of war, a threat to national security, internal political instability or any other public emergency as a justification of torture or other cruel, inhuman or degrading treatment or punishment...."*

UN Basic Principles on the Use of Force and Firearms by Law Enforcement Officials elaborates on point 3 of the UN Code, and includes the requirement that: *"(4) law enforcement officials, in carrying out their duty, shall, as far as possible, apply non-violent means before resorting to the use of force and firearms. They may use force and firearms only if other means remain ineffective...(9) Law enforcement officials shall not use firearms against persons except in self defence or defence of others against the imminent threat of death or serious injury, to prevent the perpetration of a particularly serious crime involving grave threat to life, to arrest a person presenting such a danger and resisting their authority, or to prevent his or her escape, and only where less extreme means are insufficient to achieve these objectives. In any event, intentional lethal use of firearms may only be made when strictly unavoidable in order to protect life. (10) In the circumstances provided for under principle 9, law enforcement officials shall identify themselves as such and give a clear warning of their intent to use firearms with sufficient time for the warning to be observed, unless to do so would unduly place the law enforcement officials at risk or would create a risk of death or serious* harm to other persons..." The Principles set out standards for rules and regulations governing the use of firearms, for the dispersal of unlawful assemblies, the treatment of persons in custody and for the training of law enforcement officials in the use of force.

Principles Governing Conventional Arms Transfers of the Organization for Security Cooperation in Europe stipulate that "each participating state will avoid transfers which would be likely to be used for the violation or suppression of human rights and fundamental freedoms."

3. Community Engagement

UDHR Article 26: "(2) Education shall be directed to the full development of the human personality and to the strengthening of respect for human rights and fundamental freedoms. It shall promote understanding, tolerance and friendship among all nations, racial or religious groups, and shall further the activities of the United Nations for the maintenance of peace."

UDHR Article 21: "(1) Everyone has the right to take part in the government of his or her country, directly or through freely chosen representatives. (2) Everyone has the right to equal access to public service in his country. (3) The will of the people shall be the basis of the authority of government; this will shall be expressed in periodic and genuine elections which shall be by universal and equal suffrage and shall be held by secret vote or by equivalent free voting procedures."

ILO Tripartite Declaration of Principles Concerning Multinational Enterprises and Social Policy, introduction: "Multinational corporations.....can help develop countries both economically and socially. They can also abuse this power by operating in a way that conflicts with the workers' and country's best interests."

4. Freedom from Discrimination

UDHR Article 2 : "1. Everyone is entitled to all the rights and freedoms set forth in this Declaration, without distinction of any kind, such as race, colour, sex, language, religion, political or other opinion, national or social origin, property, birth or other status. 2. Furthermore, no distinction shall be made on the basis of the political, jurisdictional or international status of the country or territory to which a person belongs, whether it be independent, trust, non-self-governing or under any other limitation of sovereignty."

ILO Convention 100: on Equal Remuneration for Men and Women Workers for Work of Equal Value.

ILO Convention 111: on Discrimination in respect of employment and occupation.

ILO Convention 165: on Workers with Family Responsibilities

5. Freedom from Slavery

UDHR Article 4: "No one shall be held in slavery or servitude; slavery and the slave trade shall be prohibited in all their forms".

ILO Conventions 29 and 105: on the Abolition of Forced or Compulsory Labour

ILO Convention 138: on the Minimum Age for Admission to Employment

6. Health and Safety

UDHR Article 3: "Everyone has the right to life, liberty and security of person." There are numerous ILO Conventions in this area. ILO Convention 155 on Occupational Safety and Health relates to general provisions, and other Conventions relate to protection in specific areas of work.

7. Freedom of Association and Right to Collective Bargaining

UDHR Article 20: "(1) Everyone has the right to freedom of peaceful assembly and association.(2) No one may be compelled to belong to an association."

UDHR Article 23: "(4) Everyone has the right to form and to join trade unions for the protection of his interests."

ILO Convention 87: on the Freedom of Association and Protection of the Right to Organise

ILO Convention 98: on the Right to Organise and Collective Bargaining

ILO Convention 135: on Workers Representatives

8. Fair working conditions

UDHR Article 23: "(1) Everyone has the right to work, to free choice of employment, to just and favourable conditions of work and to protection against unemployment. (2) Everyone, without any discrimination, has the right to equal pay for equal work. (3) Everyone who works has the right to just and favourable remuneration ensuring for himself and his family an existence worthy of human dignity, and supplemented, if necessary, by other means of social protection."

UDHR Article 24: "Everyone has the right to rest and leisure, including reasonable limitation of working hours and periodic holidays with pay."

There are numerous ILO Conventions relating to this area, including the following:

ILO Convention 95 and **131** on wages

ILO Conventions 14 and **106** on weekly rest

ILO Convention 132 on holidays with pay

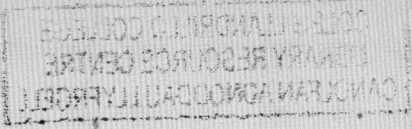

The UN Universal Declaration of Human Rights

Adopted and proclaimed by UN General Assembly on 10 December 1948

PREAMBLE

WHEREAS recognition of the inherent dignity and of the equal and inalienable rights of all members of the human family is the foundation of freedom, justice and peace in the world,

WHEREAS disregard and contempt for human rights have resulted in barbarous acts which have outraged the conscience of mankind, and the advent of a world in which human beings shall enjoy freedom of speech and belief and freedom from fear and want has been proclaimed as the highest aspiration of the common people,

WHEREAS it is essential, if man is not to be compelled to have recourse, as a last resort, to rebellion against tyranny and oppression, that human rights should be protected by the rule of law,

WHEREAS it is essential to promote the development of friendly relations between nations,

WHEREAS the peoples of the United Nations have in the Charter reaffirmed their faith in fundamental human rights, in the dignity and worth of the human person and in the equal rights of men and women and have determined to promote social progress and better standards of life in larger freedom,

WHEREAS Member States have pledged themselves to achieve, in co-operation with the United Nations, the promotion of universal respect for and observance of human rights and fundamental freedoms,

WHEREAS a common understanding of these rights and freedoms is of the greatest importance for the full realisation of this pledge,

Now, therefore, THE GENERAL ASSEMBLY proclaims this Universal Declaration of Human Rights as a common standard of achievement for all peoples and all nations, to the end that every individual and every organ of society, keeping this Declaration constantly in mind, shall strive by teaching and education to promote respect for these rights and freedoms and by progressive measures, national and international, to secure their universal and effective recognition and observance, both among the peoples of the Member States themselves and among the peoples of territories under their jurisdiction.

ARTICLE 1.
All human beings are born free and equal in dignity and rights. They are endowed with reason and conscience and should act towards one another in a spirit of brotherhood.

ARTICLE 2.
Everyone is entitled to all the rights and freedoms set forth in this Declaration, without distinction of any kind, such as race, colour, sex, language, religion, political or other opinion, national or social origin, property, birth or other status.
Furthermore, no distinction shall be made on the basis of the political, jurisdictional or international status of the country or territory to which a person belongs, whether it be independent, trust, non-self-governing or under any other limitation of sovereignty.

ARTICLE 3.
Everyone has the right to life, liberty and security of person.

ARTICLE 4.
No one shall be held in slavery or servitude; slavery and the slave trade shall be prohibited in all their forms.

ARTICLE 5.
No one shall be subjected to torture or to cruel, inhuman or degrading treatment or punishment.

ARTICLE 6.
Everyone has the right to recognition everywhere as a person before the law.

ARTICLE 7.
All are equal before the law and are entitled without any discrimination to equal protection of the law. All are entitled to equal protection against any discrimination in violation of this Declaration and against any incitement to such discrimination.

ARTICLE 8.
Everyone has the right to an effective remedy by the competent national tribunals for acts violating the fundamental rights granted him by the constitution or by law.

ARTICLE 9.
No one shall be subjected to arbitrary arrest, detention or exile.

ARTICLE 10.
Everyone is entitled in full equality to a fair and public hearing by an independent and impartial tribunal, in the determination of his rights and obligations and of any criminal charge against him.

ARTICLE 11.
(1) Everyone charged with a penal offence has the right to be presumed innocent until proved guilty according to law in a public trial at which he has had all the guarantees necessary for his defence.
(2) No one shall be held guilty of any penal offence on account of any act or omission which did not constitute a penal offence, under national or international law, at the time when it was committed. Nor shall a heavier penalty be imposed than the one that was applicable at the time the penal offence was committed.

ARTICLE 12.
No one shall be subjected to arbitrary interference with his privacy, family, home or correspondence, nor to attacks upon his honour and reputation. Everyone has the right to the protection of the law against such interference or attacks.

ARTICLE 13.
(1) Everyone has the right to freedom of movement and residence within the borders of each State.
(2) Everyone has the right to leave any country, including his own, and to return to his country.

ARTICLE 14.
(1) Everyone has the right to seek and to enjoy in other countries asylum from persecution.
(2) This right may not be invoked in the case of prosecutions genuinely arising form non-political crimes or from acts contrary to the purposes and principles of the United Nations.

ARTICLE 15.
(1) Everyone has the right to a nationality.
(2) No one shall be arbitrarily deprived of his nationality nor denied the right to change his nationality.

ARTICLE 16.
(1) Men and women of full age, without any limitation due to race, nationality or religion, have the right to marry and to found a family. They are entitled to equal rights as to marriage, during marriage and at its dissolution.
(2) Marriage shall be entered into only with the free and full consent of the intending spouses.
(3) The family is the natural and fundamental group unit of society and is entitled to protection by society and the State.

ARTICLE 17.

(1) Everyone has the right to own property alone as well as in association with others.
(2) No one shall be arbitrarily deprived of his property.

ARTICLE 18.

Everyone has the right to freedom of thought, conscience and religion; this right includes freedom to change his religion or belief, and freedom, either alone or in community with others and in public or private, to manifest his religion or belief in teaching, practice, worship and observance.

ARTICLE 19.

Everyone has the right to freedom of opinion and expression; this right includes freedom to hold opinions without interference and to seek, receive and impart information and ideas through any media and regardless of frontiers.

ARTICLE 20.

(1) Everyone has the right to freedom of peaceful assembly and association.
(2) No one may be compelled to belong to an association.

ARTICLE 21.

(1) Everyone has the right to take part in the government of his country, directly or through chosen representatives.
(2) Everyone has the right of equal access to public service in his country.
(3) The will of the people shall be the basis of the authority of government; this will shall be expressed in periodic and genuine elections which shall be held by universal and equal suffrage and shall be held by secret vote or by equivalent free voting procedures.

ARTICLE 22.

Everyone, as a member of society, has the right to social security and is entitled to realisation, through national effort and international co-operation and in accordance with the organisation and resources of each State, of the economic, social and cultural rights indispensable for his dignity and the free development of his personality.

ARTICLE 23.

(1) Everyone has the right to work, to free choice of employment, to just and favourable conditions of work and to protection against unemployment.
(2) Everyone, without any discrimination, has the right to equal pay for equal work.
(3) Everyone has the right to just and favourable remuneration ensuring for himself and his family an existence worthy of human dignity, and supplemented, if necessary, by other means of social protection.
(4) Everyone has the right to form and to join trade unions for the protection of his interests.

ARTICLE 24.

Everyone has the right to rest and leisure, including reasonable limitation of working hours and periodic holidays with pay.

ARTICLE 25.

(1) Everyone has the right to a standard of living adequate for the health and well-being of himself and of his family, including food, clothing, housing and medical care and necessary social services, and the right to security in the event of unemployment, sickness, disability, widowhood, old age and other lack of livelihood in circumstances beyond his control.
(2) Motherhood and childhood are entitled to special care and assistance. All children, whether born in or out of wedlock, shall enjoy the same social protection.

ARTICLE 26.

(1) Everyone has the right to education. Education shall be free, at least in the elementary and fundamental stages. Elementary education shall be compulsory. Technical and professional education shall be made generally available and higher education shall be equally accessible to all on the basis of merit.
(2) Education shall be directed to the full development of the human personality and to the strengthening of respect for human rights and fundamental freedoms. It shall promote understanding, tolerance and friendship among all nations, racial or religious groups, and shall further the activities of the United Nations for the maintenance of peace.
(3) Parents have a prior right to choose the kind of education that shall be given their children.

ARTICLE 27.

(1) Everyone has the right to freely participate in the cultural life of the community, to enjoy the arts and to share in scientific advancement and its benefits.
(2) Everyone has the right to the protection of the moral and material interests resulting from any scientific, literary or artistic production of which he is the author.

ARTICLE 28.

Everyone is entitled to a social and international order in which the rights and freedoms set forth in this Declaration can be fully realised.

ARTICLE 29.

(1) Everyone has duties to the community in which alone the free and full development of is personality is possible.
(2) In the exercise of his rights and freedoms, everyone shall be subject only to such limitations as are determined by law solely for the purpose of securing due recognition and respect for the rights and freedoms of others and of meeting the just requirements of morality, public order and the general welfare in a democratic society.
(3) These rights and freedoms may in no case be exercised contrary to the purposes and principles of the United Nations.

ARTICLE 30.

Nothing in this Declaration may be interpreted as implying for any State, group or person any right to engage in any activity or to perform any act aimed at the destruction of any of the rights and freedoms set forth herein.

RESOURCES – NGOs and others

Amnesty International UK Business Group
99-119 Rosebery Avenue
London EC1R 4RE
UK
Tel: 44 (0) 207 417 6382
www.amnesty.org.uk/business

Anti-Slavery International
The Stableyard
Broomgrove Rd.
London SW9 9TL
UK
Tel: 44 (0) 207 501 8920
www.antislavery.org

Ashridge Centre for Business and Society
Ashridge Management College
Ashridge
Berkhamsted
Herts HP4 1NS
UK
Tel: 44 (0) 1442 841174
www.ashridge.org.uk

Business In The Community (BITC)
44 Baker Street
London W1M 1DH
UK
Tel: 44 (0) 207 224 1600
www.bitc.org.uk
www.business-impact.org.uk
(includes information on business and human rights)

Business For Social Responsibility (BSR)
609 Mission St., 2nd Floor
San Francisco, CA, 94105
USA
Tel: (415) 537 0888
www.bsr.org

Calvert Group – U.S. socially responsible investment
company
4550 Montgomery Avenue
Bethesda,
Maryland 20814
USA
Tel: 1-800- 368-2748
www.calvertgroup.com

Control Risks Group – *A security and risk assessment consultancy body*
83 Victoria Street
London SW1H 0HW
UK
Tel: 44 (0) 207 222 1552/ 388 1187
www.crg.com

Corporate Watch *is an online magazine documenting the social, political, economic and environmental impacts of corporate activity.*
P.O. Box 29344
San Francisco, CA 94129
USA
Tel: (415) 561 6568
www.igc.org/trac/

Council on Economic Priorities
30 Irving Place
New York, NY 10003-2386
USA
Tel: (212) 420-1133
www.cepnyc.org

Council on Economic Priorities Accreditation Agency (CEPAA)
has developed the SA8000 code, which is a comprehensive and global system of standards embodying human rights principles
30 Irving Place
New York, NY 10003
USA
tel: (212) 358 7697
www.cepaa.org

The Danish Centre for Human Rights *is working with the Confederation of Danish Industries on a human rights impact assessment project*
38 Studiestraede
DK-1455 Copenhagen K
Denmark
Tel: 45 33 30 88 00
www.humanrights.dk

EIRIS (The Ethical Investment Research Service)
80-84 Bondway
London SW8 1SF
UK
Tel: 44 (0)20 7840 5700
www.eiris.u-net.com

Ethical Trading Initiative (ETI)
78-79 Long Lane
London EC1A 9EX
UK
Tel: 44 (0) 207 796 0515
www.ethicaltrade.org

Global Exchange *is a non-profit research and action centre, dedicated to promoting environmental, political and social justice around the world. It focuses on U.S. corporations*
2017 Mission Street No. 303
San Francisco, California 94110
USA
Tel: (415) 255 7296
www.globalexchange.org

Global Witness
P.O. Box 6042
London N19 5WP
UK
Tel: 44 (0) 207 272 6731
www.oneworld.org/globalwitness

Human Rights Watch
Human Rights Watch (UK)
33 Islington High St.
London N1 9LH
UK
Tel: 44 (0) 207 713 1995

Human Rights Watch (US)
350 Fifth Avenue, 34th Floor
New York, NY 10118-3299
USA
Tel: (212) 290 4700
www.hrw.org

Institute of Social and Ethical Accountability *is a professional body which promotes best practice in social and ethical accounting, auditing and reporting*
Thrale House
44-46 Southwark St
London SE1 1UN
UK
Tel: 44 (0) 207 407 7370
www.AccountAbility.org.uk

ICFTU – International Confederation of Free Trade Unions
5 Boulevard du Roi Albert II
Bte 1
B-1210 Brussels
Belgium
Tel: 32 2 224 0211
www.icftu.org

International Federation of Chemical, Energy, Mine and General Workers' Union (ICEM) *is a global industrial trade union federation representing more than 20 million workers worldwide. It is developing a general code of practice on labour and human rights*
Avenue Emile de Béco 109
B-1050 Brussels
Belgium
Tel: 32 2 6262020
www.icem.org

Lawyers Committee For Human Rights (LCHR)
333 Seventh Ave., 13th Floor
New York
NY, 10001-5004
USA
Tel: (212) 845 52656
(415) 674 4024
www.lchr.org

New Economics Foundation
Cinnamon House
6-8 Cole Street
London SE1 4YH
UK
Tel: 44 (0) 207 407 7447
www.neweconomics.org

Norwegian Confederation of Business and Industry (NHO)
Middelthunsgate 27
PO Box 5250 Majorstua 0303
Oslo
Norway
Tel: 47 23 08 80 00
www.nho.no

OXFAM GB
274 Banbury Road
Oxford OX 2 7DZ
UK
Tel: 44 (0) 1865 311 311
www.oxfam.org.uk

Pension Investment Research Consultants (PIRC) –
UK investment adviser to institutional investors on corporate governance and corporate responsibility issue.
4th Floor, Cityside
40 Adler Street
Lonon E1 1EE
UK
Tel: 44 (0) 207 247 2323
www.pirc.co.uk

The Prince of Wales Business Leaders Forum
15-16 Cornwall Terrace
Regent's Park
London NW1 4QP
UK
Tel: 44 (0) 207 467 3600
www.pwblf.org

Save The Children Fund (UK)
17 Grove Lane
London SE5 8RD
UK
Tel: 44 (0) 207 703 5400
www.savethechildren.org.uk

Sweatshop Watch
310 Eighth St., Suite 309
Oakland, CA 94607
USA
Tel: (510) 834 8990
www.sweatshopwatch.org

Traidcraft – *UK independent fair trade organisation.*
Kingsway
Gateshead
Tyne & Wear NE11 0NE
UK
Tel: 44 (0)191 491 0591
www.traidcraft.co.uk

Transparency International – *an international NGO dedicated to combating corruption through building coalitions between state, civil society and the private sector*
Transparency International e.V.
Otto-Suhr-Allee 97-99
D-10585 Berlin
Germany
Tel: 49 30 34 38 20 0
www. transparency.de

World Monitors – *Business and Human Rights Consulting*
450 Lexington Avenue
Suite 3800
New York
NY 10017
USA
Tel: (212) 551 2637
www.worldmonitors.com

RESOURCES –Inter-governmental organisations

OECD – The Organisation for Economic Co-operation and Development
2, Rue Andre Pascal
F-75775 Paris Cedex 16
France
Tel: 33 1 45 24 80 90
www.oecd.fr

International Labour Organisation (ILO)
CH-1211 Geneva 22
Switzerland
Fax: 41 22 799 6938
www.ilo.org

UNICEF
UNICEF House
3 United Nations Plaza
New York, NY 10017
USA
www.unicef.org

UN Office of the High Commissioner For Human Rights
8-14 Avenue de la Paix
1211 Geneva 10
Switzerland
Tel: 41 22 917 9000
www.unhchr.ch

UN Global Compact
United Nations
New York, NY 10017
USA
Tel: (212) 963 8302
www.unglobalcompact.org

BP Amoco
BP Amoco plc
Britannic House
1 Finsbury Circus
London EC2M 7BA
UK
Tel: 44 (0) 207 496 4000
www.bpamoco.com/about/policies/ethic.htm

B&Q
B&Q plc
1 Hampshire Corporate Park
Chandlers Ford
Eastleigh, Hants SO53 3YX
UK
Tel: 44 (0)1703 256 148
www.diy.co.uk

Levi Strauss & Co
Levi Strauss & Co
P.O. Box 7215
San Francisco, CA, 94120
USA
Tel: (415) 501-6000
www.levistrauss.com

Pentland Group
Pentland Group plc
Pentland Centre
Lakeside
Squires Lane, Finchley
London N3 2QL
UK
Tel: 44 (0) 208 346 2600
www.pentland.com

Reebok
Reebok International Ltd
100 Technology Center Drive
Stoughton
MA 02072
USA
Tel: (781) 401 5000
www.reebok.com/human_rights.html

Rio Tinto
Rio Tinto plc
6 St James's Square
London SW1Y 4LD
UK
Tel: 44 (0) 207 930 2399
www.riotinto.com

Shell
Shell International Ltd.
Shell Centre
4-8 York Road
London SE1 7NA
UK
Tel: 44 (0) 207 934 4134
www.shell.com/principles/general

WMC Resources
WMC Resources Ltd.
Head office
60 City Road Southbank
VIC, 3006
AUSTRALIA
Tel: 61 3 96856000
www.wmc.com.au

Publications

Human Rights from the Perspective of Business and Industry –
A Checklist
Confederation of Norwegian Business and Industry (NHO) (1999)
Tel: (47) 23 08 80 00

....

Business and Human Rights in a Time of Change
Christopher Avery
Amnesty International UK (2000)
Tel: 44 (0) 207 417 6382

....

Human Rights Standards and the Responsibility of
Transnational Corporations
Michael K. Addo (ed)
Kluwer Law International (1999)

....

Amnesty International Report 2000
Amnesty International
(June 2000) www.amnesty.org

....

Human Rights Watch World Report 2000
Human Rights Watch
www.hrw.org

....

Benchmarks for multinational companies reporting on human and
labour rights (draft)
Amnesty International USA, Human Rights Watch, Council on
Economic Priorities, PricewaterhouseCoopers (January 2000)
This is a draft paper defining categories, aspects and indicators that
companies can use in measuring and reporting on human rights in
the workplace. It is part of the Global Reporting Initiative.
Jennifer Woodward, Reputation Assurance Services, PWC London
Tel: 44 (0) 207 804 1871
Anne Weiss, PWC New York
Tel: (212) 596 7892

....

Stitching Footballs: Voices of Children in Sialkot, Pakistan
Rachel Marcus & David Husselbee
Save the Children Fund UK and UNICEF (1997)
Tel: 44 (0) 207 708 2508

....

What Works for Working Children
Jo Boyden, Birgitta Ling & William Myers
Save The Children UK and UNICEF (1998)
Tel: 44 (0) 207 703 5400

....

"Don't pull out, put in" – a guide to responsible business
approaches to child labour
Fional King and Rachel Marcus,
Save the Children Fund UK (May 2000)
Tel: 44 (0) 207 703 5400

The Business of Peace – a research report on the role of
companies in conflict situations. (2000)
Jane Nelson, The Prince of Wales Business Leaders Forum, with
International Alert and CEP.
Tel: 44 (0) 207 467 3600

....

The Price of Oil: Corporate Responsibility and Human Rights
Violations in Nigeria's Oil Producing Communities
Human Rights Watch (1999)
Tel: 44 (0) 207 713 1995

....

Angola Unravels: The Rise and Fall of the Lusaka Peace Process
Human Rights Watch (1999)
Tel: 44 (0) 207 713 1995

....

Business and Human Rights:
A Management Primer
Shell International Petroleum Company (SIPC) (1998)
Tel: 44 (0) 207 934 6704

....

Oxfam Business Pack – an interactive resource pack for
companies looking at issues of ethical sourcing
Oxfam GB (2000)
Tel: 44 (0) 1865 312245l

....

Standards of Corporate Social Responsibility
Social Venture Network (SVN) (1999)
Tel: (415) 561 6501

....

Starter Pack on Social Responsibility
Business in the Community (BITC) (2000)
Tel: 44 (0) 207 224 1600

....

Building Corporate Accountability
Simon Zadek, Peter Pruzan and Richard Evans; Earthscan
publications (1997)
Tel: 44 (0)20 7278 0433

....

Cannibals with Forks: the Triple Bottom Line of 21st Century
Business
John Elkington; Capstone Publishing (1997)
Tel: 44 (0) 1865 798623

....

Integrating Social Concerns into Private Sector Decision-making – A
Review of Corporate Practices in the Mining, Oil and Gas Sectors
World Bank Discussion Paper no.384 (1998) Kathryn McPhail and
Aidan Davy

When Good Companies do Bad Things: Responsibility and Risk in an Age of Globalisation
P. Schwartz and B. Gibb, New York,
John Wiley & Sons (1999)

....

Principles for Global Corporate Responsibility: Benchmarks for Measuring Business Performance
Interfaith Center on Corporate Responsibility (ICCR)
Tel: (212) 870 2293

....

Ethical Performance
(monthly UK newsletter for socially responsible business)
Dunstans Publishing
Tel: 44 (0)1227 472 610

....

Human Rights Guidelines for Companies
Amnesty International UK (1998)
Tel: 44 (0) 207 417 6382

....

Frameworks for Human Rights,
New Economics Foundation (2000)
Tel: 44 (0) 207 407 7447

Alphabetical Index

A

B

C

H

Human Rights Watch   26,46,96

I-K

India   60,109
indigenous peoples' rights   48-51
   compensation   49-50
   forced relocation   49
   guidelines for companies   14,50
   ILO Convention No.169   14,49
   WMC Resources case study   51,98-101
Indonesia   30,54,103,116-117
Institute of Social and Ethical Accountability   78
Interfaith Center on Corporate Responsibility   68
International Confederation of Free Trade Unions (ICFTU)   53,55,115
International Covenant on Civil and Political Rights   13,22-23
International Covenant on Economic, Cultural and Social Rights   22-23
International Federation of Chemical, Energy,Mines and
               General Workers' Unions (ICEM)   117
international human rights standards   8,22-24,28
international law   22-23
International Labour Organisation (ILO)
   Convention No.29 on Forced Labour   60
   Convention No.131 on Minimum Wage Fixing   58-59
   Convention No.169 on Indigenous and Tribal Peoples   49
   core standards   11,22,28,52,56
   Declaration on Fundamental Principles and Rights at Work   79
   role of   79
   supervisory system   79
International Textile Garment and Leather Workers Federation   104,120
Internet   9,22
   power of   73
Intranet   113

L

labour rights   (see also bonded and forced labour, child labour
                 and freedom of association)
   B& Q case study on working conditions   59, 109-111
   civil and political rights of trade unionists   55
   guidelines for companies   15-18,52-61
   ILO core conventions   28,52,56
land rights (see indigenous peoples' rights)
legal jurisdiction over companies   79-80
letter of assurance   30
Levi Strauss   66
   case study on multi-stakeholder partnerships   118-120
London Stock Exchange listing requirements   26,82

M

migrant workers   60
Multilateral Agreement on Investment (MAI)   73
Myanmar   22,72-74,81
   forced labour   61

N

O

P-Q

R

S